OUTLINE GRAMMAR

OF THE

KACHARI (BARA) LANGUAGE

OUTLINE GRAMMAR

OF THE

KACHARI (BARA) LANGUAGE

AS SPOKEN IN

DISTRICT DARRANG, ASSAM;

With Illustrative Sentences, Notes, Reading Lessons, and a Short Vocabulary.

By REV S. ENDLE

GYAN

Published by

Gyan Publishing House
5, Ansari Road
Daryaganj, New Delhi-110002
Phone: 011-47034999, 9811692060
E-mail: books@gyanbooks.com

Distribution Network
gyanbooks.com
India, USA, Canada, UK, Australia

ISBN: 978-93-6280-013-8 (HB)
First Published, 1884

2nd Impression 2024

Printed at: Gyan Press, Delhi.

OUTLINE GRAMMAR OF THE KACHARI (BARA) LANGUAGE
Author: REV S. ENDLE

OUTLINE GRAMMAR

OF THE

KACHÁRI (BÅṚÅ) LANGUAGE

AS SPOKEN IN

DISTRICT DARRANG, ASSAM;

With Illustrative Sentences, Notes, Reading Lessons, and a short Vocabulary.

BY REV. S. ENDLE,
S. P. G. ASSAM CHURCH MISSION, LATE STUDENT, ST. AUGUSTINE'S COLLEGE, CANTERBURY.

SHILLONG:
PRINTED AT THE ASSAM SECRETARIAT PRESS.

1884.

PREFACE.

THE following brief sketch of the Kachári language as spoken in this district (Darrang) has been put together under many difficulties and disadvantages, as the writer has been able to give to its compilation little more than mere scraps and fragments of his time. Much of the Accidence, in particular, was drawn up in MS. some two years since, and should have been re-written before publication, had the pressure of other duties given opportunity for so doing; for it was put together at various times and in different places, and the whole suffers from a want of re-arrangement and expansion. This is especially the case with the section which treats of Verbs, and the peculiar way in which they are compounded with other parts of speech; *i.e.*, with nouns, adjectives, and other verbal roots. There are many points of interest, too, in the language, *e.g.*, the exact use and force of the tenses, which must still be regarded as open questions, and with regard to which we shall not perhaps be in a position to speak with anything like authority until we know something of the Grammar of the many closely cognate languages. But as there seems little prospect of any great additions being made to our knowledge in this direction for some time to come, it seems best on the whole to allow the following pamphlet to appear at once, with all its obvious and manifold imperfections. As it stands it fairly represents the speech of the Kachári population of this district, as gathered from the lips of the people themselves during the last fifteen or twenty years;

and it may at least serve to assist and lighten the labours of other workers in the same field of research—a field which certainly cannot be said to be exhausted, or in any real sense to have been at all adequately cultivated as yet.

A further reason for at once publishing the following Outline Grammar, in spite of its many shortcomings, is supplied by the desire to have a Manual of this kind for the use of managers of tea-factories, &c. The Kacháris are essentially the navvies of Assam,—a nation of "hewers of wood and drawers of water," and much of the hard physical work (hoeing, jungle-clearing, &c.) on tea-factories is still carried on by them. The manager of any factory on which Kachári labourers are employed in largo numbers, will certainly find it to his interest to learn something of their language; for they are an intensely *clannish* people, and are not a little gratified by seeing their employer show some interest in their customs, language, and manner of life. The writer well remembers a little "scene" in a factory in this district (Darrang), where a number of Kachári labourers, who had taken umbrage at some real or fancied grievance, suddenly came up to the manager's bungalow, threw down their hoes, &c., before him in a highly theatrical, demonstrative fashion, and with the great plainness of speech Kacháris are apt to use at such times, announced that they were going off to their own distant homes forthwith. A few simple, humourous words addressed to them, partly in their own tongue, soon made them see the absurdity of the position they were assuming; and after a short colloquy they took up their hoes and went back to their lines in great good humour. Many managers complain of Kachári labourers as being difficult to get on with—and certainly they have no small share of doggedness; and when once their suspicions have been aroused, with or without reason, it is not at all easy to bring them to a happier state of mind. But if they are not to be easily *driven*, they can be very easily *led;* and undoubtedly one of the most powerful influences which their employer can bring to bear upon them, is to be found in a command of their national form of speech, to which (as to all else that is national or clannish) they are very strongly attached. Few things are more pleasing than to see the flush of real pleasure and intelligence which passes over the dull, heavy, expressionless features of the Kachári's countenance on being addressed in his own mother tongue. And if one of the highest forms of human pleasure consists in giving innocent pleasure to *others*, any European, whose life's work has to be done in Assam, and who will take the trouble to acquire some knowledge of this form of non-Áryan speech, will rarely be at a loss to make this pleasure his own.

Wide range of Kachári family of languages.

The limited extent to which this language and its cognate tongues have been hitherto studied, is the more to be regretted, as there is great reason to believe that it was at one time widely spoken over a great portion of the Brahmaputra Valley, as well as in the adjoining districts of north-east Bengal. Much light is thrown on this subject by the information given in the "Report on the Census of Assam for 1881," pages 67—82. We find it there stated that the race known to us under various names (Boḍo, Gáro, &c.) constitutes at least one-third of the population of the Assam Valley; and this statement is probably well within the mark. The Deori Chutias, who are found so far east as Sadiya, are said to speak a language closely akin to Kachári, though no Outline Grammar of their speech has hitherto been published. Mr. Lyall (*see* "Census Report," pages 78—81) gives reason for suspecting that the Mikirs may be an outlying branch of the great Boḍo family, though this must perhaps be still regarded as an open question. And there is reason to think that the Kacháris were at one time the dominant race, or at least one of the dominant races, in the Brahmaputra Valley; and as such they seem to have left traces of their language in the names of some of the most prominent physical features of the country. Thus the names of many of the principal rivers of Assam begin with the syllable, "Dí," which is perhaps the Kachári word ("dŭí," "dí") for "water," *e.g.*, Dí-hong, Dí-bong, Dí-bru, Dí-hing, Dí-sáng, Dí-khu, Dí-soi, Dí-ju, Dí-mu, Dí-mangal, Dí-krang, Dí-kurai, Dí-putá, Dí-má gasum ("black water"), Dí-ang, &c., (*cf.* Dimápur— Dŭímápúr, *i.e.*, River-town, the old Kachári capital on the Dhansiri River). But however this may be, the evidence of language points clearly to the conclusion that the peoples known to us as Kacháris (Boṛo, Boḍo, Bâṛâ), Mêch, Hojai, Hojang, Gáros, Dhímáls, &c., are one and the same race, and still speak what is essentially the same form of non-Áryan speech. To these must be added the Koch, Rájbansis, Mahalia, Phulgorias, Rábhás, and others, most of whom have lost the use of their old mother tongue, and have to a greater or less degree fallen under the influence of Hinduism. A hurried examination of the "Specimens of the Languages of India" (published at the Bengal Secretariat Press, 1874), pages 186—217, has led me to the conclusion that even the language there described as "Hill Tipperá" has very much in common with the Kachári of Darrang, and may indeed be regarded as virtually the same form of speech. (Some evidence pointing in this direction is given in a short list of words and inflections on a later page). This, if it can be established, is interesting, as it would prove that the Kachári race extends so far to the south and west as to cross the Surmá Valley—so that this language would seem to be still a living tongue for people so widely scattered as the Deori Chutias near Sadiya and the dwellers on the Tipperá Hills of Eastern Bengal. In Western Darrang, North Kámrup, and Goálpára, and in the Duár country stretching away from near Tezpur towards Jalpaiguri and Dárjíling, the Kacháris under various names form the great bulk of the population; and it is possible that they may be akin to many of the races occupying the hills to the south of the Surmá Valley, though it is not easy to speak with any kind of authority on this part of the subject until we have Outline Grammars, or at least full Vocabularies and typical sentences illustrating the languages of these last-mentioned races, so as to furnish the means of making a comparison between these various forms of speech.

Various names.

This people, who once occupied so large a portion of North-East India, and who still constitute at least one-third of the population of the Brahmaputra Valley, are known to us vaguely as Kacháris, but they rarely, it ever, use this name among themselves. In Western Darrang and North Kámrúp, they they very commonly speak of themselves as "Bâṛâ" (Bâḍâ, Boṛo, Boḍo) or "Bâṛâ físá" (= "children of the Bâṛâ"), and this title seems to be largely used by them in North-East Bengal. In Goálpára they are commonly known as Mêch (Mês)—a designation I have never known applied to them in this district. In all likelihood this name was given to them in contempt by their Hindu neighbours—("Mlêch," "Mlêchchha"=outcast, barbarian, &c.) At the foot of the Gáro Hills they are known as Hojai and Hájong,—a name probably equivalent to "hillmen" ("Háju; házu"=hill, in Kachári; "áchu," in Gáro; "háchuk," in Hill Tipperá). In Naugáon, where also Hojai Kacháris are found, a local name, "Lálung," is commonly used—a term of wholly unknown etymology. From information obligingly placed at my disposal by the officer in charge of the North Kachár Hills (Mr. Soppitt), it would seem that the Kacháris of that part speak of themselves as "Dŭímá-sá," *i.e.*, "the people of the great river" (*cf.* the name of the old Kachári centre on the Dhansiri, Dŭímá-pur,—the town on the big river,—Riverton); and with this may be connected another local name for Kacháris, *i.e.*, "Dhímál" (Dŭímál?)—a name never applied to them in this district. On the whole, putting together two of the groups of names used by themselves ;—(1) "Hojai" and "Hájong," *i.e.*, "hillmen," and (2) "Dŭímá-sá" and "Dhimál," *i.e.*, "men of the big river," they would seem to look upon themselves as "men of the mountain and the flood,"—as Highlanders, in contra-distinction to the people of the plains. This theory would seem to be borne out by what we see now; for they are still found in large numbers in the neighbourhood of *rivers*, *e.g.*, the Dhansiri, Kopili, &c., and the terai country lying at varying distances from the foot of the *hills* from near Tezpur towards Dárjiling, which tract of country is abundantly watered by a vast number of small *rivers* (dŭí-sá). They still show also a distinct preference for high land as a dwelling-place; some members of this widely-spread race, *e.g.*, Gáros, the people of Hill Tipperá, Mikirs (?), &c., actually live on the hills; whilst others, who have taken up their abode in the plains (Hojai, Hájong, the Kacháris of Darrang), live for the most part at no great distance from the hills; and I have observed that wherever high land is obtainable for building, the Kachári settler almost invariably fixes his dwelling there.

Suggestions.

The time has perhaps come when a definite attempt should be made to obtain more light than we now possess on the comparative ethnology and linguistic affinities of the numerous tribes on this North-Eastern Frontier. Something was done in this direction by the publication of the "Specimens of Languages of India," under the auspices of Sir G. Campbell some ten years since (1874). But the usefulness of this work for all the purposes of comparative philology, is very greatly marred by the numerous errors in spelling which disfigure its pages. It might be well perhaps to re-issue this work after a thorough revision, the contributors all carefully using the same symbols on a system to be settled beforehand for representing the same, or similar, sounds; or, it should surely be possible, for a competent body of philologists to draw up a list of words and inflections and typical sentences, so contrived and arranged as to bring to the front in bold relief the more salient features of the different languages concerned. But, above all, the compilation of *Outline Grammars* of the different languages should be systematically encouraged. Such Grammars, however rudimentary and incomplete they might be, could hardly fail to throw much light on various difficult questions of comparative philology, if they included (as they should do) a careful treatment of words in every-day use, the inflections of nouns, the conjugation of verbs,—this latter part of speech (the verb) being treated with especial clearness and fulness in its different forms; *e.g.*, the Active, Passive, Negative, Causative, Inceptive, and Completive forms. Compound verbs especially should receive particular attention, as helping to throw light on the genius of each language and its system of word-building. No less an authority than Professor Max Müller has told us that it is to the *inflectional* part of a language (its declension of nouns, conjugation of verbs, &c., &c.), rather than to its *vocabulary*, that we should look, if we would get any true insight into its real character and its relation to other forms of speech; and therefore, while lists of words carefully written down on a pre-arranged system have an undoubted value of their own, it is still more important that the

Accidence and Syntactical conditions of a language should receive close attention and be prominently brought to the front if the Ethnology and Comparative Philology of this part of India are to have thrown upon them the light of which they stand so greatly in need. I speak of "this part of India" in particular, because Assam, with its immense variety of languages, offers an especially wide and rich field to the philological student—a field which has yielded some valuable results already, though it has never yet been at all adequately cultivated. A tea-planter of somewhat sarcastic temperament once remarked in the writer's presence that the "Tower of Babel must have been somewhere within the limits of Assam." This assertion is perhaps hardly to be defended on historical or geographical grounds; but whoever has listened—perhaps without being much edified thereby—to the medley of tongues spoken at an Assamese Mêlá, or even on a large tea-factory, will not be slow to admit that the planter's remark was not entirely without some show of justification. But this very medley of tongues, which puts great difficulties at once in the path of the Magistrate, the Missionary, the Administrator, and the Planter, offers a promising field of labour to the student of language, whose privilege it may be to evolve something like order and harmony out of what has hitherto been little better than a philological chaos. The demands made upon him by the duties of a busy life, involving frequent absence from head-quarters, as well as a regard for his Ordination Vows, not to mention other reasons, will prevent the present writer from giving much time and labour to researches of this kind; but to those who have the leisure, the ability, and the will for the work, the field is one full of promise. For the better we understand the *languages* of these simple peoples, the better we shall understand the people themselves—their hopes, fears, wishes, aspirations, and all that helps to make up the sum of their simple lives from day to day; the better, too, we shall understand and value the many virtues (honesty, truthfulness, simplicity, straightforwardness, &c.), which, in spite of a rough, uninviting exterior, many of these tribes do undoubtedly possess; the greater, too, will be our power of *sympathizing* with them, and so of lifting them up to a sense of the higher and better things we ourselves enjoy, and ought to be anxious to see them share with us.

S. ENDLE.

CAMP BENGBÁRI, DARRANG, *24th May 1884.*

In the following pages the student is not to expect absolute uniformity in the use of accents and other diacritical marks, or even in the spelling of words. Many discrepancies and inconsistencies in this respect will doubtless be found; and of these some are, of course, due to carelessness or oversight on the writer's part; but there are others which are not unintentional. The fact is that, with our present knowledge of the language, the exact pronunciation, and even the correct spelling, of certain words, cannot be fixed with certainty. This is true even of words in common, every-day use, *e.g.*, the word for "good." The usual form of this word in Kachári is "gằhàm;" but it sometimes appears as "gàhàm," "gahàm," "ghàm," or even as "hàm" (the first syllable being elided.) There are also curious dialectic differences in localities within a few miles of each other; thus, the common words for "cow" and "tiger" here (Bengbári) are "mosaú" and "mosá:" whilst at Sámábári and Mangalbásá, some fifteen or twenty miles to the south, these words appear as "mokhaú" and "mokhá," the medial sibilant letter being replaced by a guttural aspirate. These are but examples of variations and dialectic differences which undoubtedly exist on a large scale; and with our present limited knowledge of Kachári and its cognate languages, it is hardly possible to decide which form of any given word of this class should be adopted as the standard for future use. So long, therefore, as the true sound and correct spelling of words of this class remains uncertain and undefined, it seems only reasonable that the method of representing these words on paper should share in this uncertainty and indefiniteness, though it may be hoped that the time will come when a closer study and a more accurate knowledge of this and the cognate languages will enable us to get rid of much of this uncertainty. The inconsistencies in the use of accents, spelling, &c., will no doubt appear sufficiently unpleasing to the scientific eye and the critical mind; but they will nevertheless fulfil a not unimportant end of their own, *i.e.*, they will help to guard the learner against supposing that he is always to hear exactly the same sound for the same word from the lips of people with whom he may attempt to hold converse. There is, however, one class of words with regard to which the writer has endeavoured to be as accurate as possible—those words where the misplacement of an accent would altogether alter the meaning; *e.g.*, "găthaú" is "deep," but "gătháu" is "sweet;" "gí-á" is the negative form of the verb "gí-nŭ," to fear (fears not), but "gŭí-á" is the negative substantive verb, is not (are not.) In dealing with words of this class some pains have been taken to secure accuracy in the use of the accents, &c.; and the writer ventures to hope that instances of their incorrect use in words of this character will be found to be but few and far between.—S. E.

The compiler very gladly takes this opportunity of expressing his deep sense of obligation to the officer in charge of the Secretariat Press for the neatness and accuracy with which the work of printing this pamphlet has been carried out. When it is remembered that the MS. was put together in a most hurried and imperfect way, and that much of the written matter deals with a language (Kachári) of which presumably those in charge of the Press knew little or nothing, it is a matter of surprise and thankfulness that the mistakes and misprints are so few and unimportant. That this result has been brought about so satisfactorily, in spite of difficulties arising from the free use of accents and various diacritical marks, reflects great credit on all concerned in the printing of the work, and to them the writer here thankfully records his obligations for their painstaking care and forethought.—S. E.

NOTE ON THE RELATION OF THE KACHÁRI (BÅṚÅ) LANGUAGE TO THAT OF HILL TIPPERÁ.

In the foregoing Preface it is pointed out that the Kachári language has much in common with that of Hill Tipperá, so much so that the two forms of speech may perhaps be regarded as simply different dialects of what is essentially the same language. It is probable that much intercourse at one time took place between the Kacháris of the Upper Dhansiri Valley (Dŭímápur) and the people of Hill Tipperá, and we know that the ruling families of the two peoples were closely related in blood. Indeed, the use of the term "Kachári," as applied to the Båṛå race by their Hindu neighbours, is commonly believed to have originated in the fact that the Rájá of Hill Tippera, when giving his daughter in marriage to the Kachári Rájá of Dŭímápur, gave as her dowry what is now the district of Kachár, which had hitherto been a part of his dominions, the Båṛå race thenceforth being known to their Hindu and Massalmán neighbours by the name of the Province (Kachár) over which their Rájá was known to rule. But however this may be, there can be little doubt that the two languages stand in very close relation to each other, and as this relationship seems not to have been prominently brought to the front hitherto, a short list of words in every-day use is here given in Kachári and Hill Tipperá, from which it will appear that many points of resemblance undoubtedly exist, which hardly admit of being explained away as merely accidental. In some cases the Gáro equivalent of a word or phrase is also given, as this is one of the most important members of the Kachári family of languages, and the Gáro word sometimes apparently forms a link between the Kachári of this district (Darrang) and the language of Hill Tipperá.

English		*Kachári.*		*Gáro.*		*Hill Tipperá.*
One	...	Sè* (sŭí)	...	Sá (shá*)	...	Kai-chhá.*
Two	...	Nè (nŭí)	...	Gni	...	Kú-núi.
Three	...	Thàm	...	Githàm	...	Kà-thàm.
Four	...	Brè (brŭí)	...	Bri	...	Búrúi.
Five	...	Bá	...	Bangá	...	Bá.
Six	...	Ṛâ (ḍâ)	...	Dak	...	Dok.
Seven	...	Sni (sĭní*)	...	Sni*	...	Chhini.*
Eight	...	Zàt*	...	Chet*	...	Chát.*
Nine	...	Skhô*	...	Skhu*	...	Chiku.*
Ten	...	Zi (zŭ*)	...	Chi (chikhung*)		Chi.*
Foot	...	Áphá	...	Jáfá	...	Yak-phá.
Eye	...	Megan	...	Mikran	...	Makoy.
Mouth	...	Khugá	...	Khusuk	...	Khúk.
Hair	...	Khenai	...	Khini (khni)	...	Khanai.
Head	...	Khâṛâ	...	Skho	...	Khorok.
Tongue	...	Silai	...	Slai	...	Chhelai.
Back	...	Bikhung	...	....		Phikhung.
Brother (elder)		Ádá	...	Ádá	...	Átá.
Child	...	Fĭsá	...	Bĭsá	...	Chhá.
Son	...	Fĭsá-zălá (child-male.)		....		Chhá-jalá (child-male.)

* The resemblance in these and like words is much closer than appears at first sight; for the Kacháris of Darrang, whose vocabulary is here written out *phonetically*, find a difficulty in uttering the sounds "cha" (chha) and "ja" (jha), and substitute for them the sibilants "s" and "z." Hence Kachári words and syllables beginning with "s" and "j" would perhaps be more correctly spelt with "ch" (chha) and "ja" (jha)—a change which would make them much more closely resemble the corresponding words in Gáro and Hill Tipperá. The principle embodied in this remark holds good throughout the entire pamphlet, and should always be borne in mind whenever it may be consulted for the purposes of Comparative Philology and Ethnology.

English.	*Kachári.*	*Gáro.*	*Hill Tipperá.*
Daughter	Fisá-zŭ (child-female.)	Bisá-mechik (child-female.)	Chhá-juk (child-female.)
God, spirit (*bhút*).	Modai	Mite	Matái.
Sun	Sán	Sál	Sál.
Star	Háthorkhi	....	Áthukuri.
Fire	Áṭ	....	Hor.
Water	Dŭí	Chi	Túi.
House	Nŭ	Nak	Nok.
Cow	Masaú	Máchu	Masu.
Dog	Sŭímá	....	Suimá.
Bird	Dáu	Dau	Táo-sá.
Hill, mountain	Házu	Áchu	Háchuk.
Tree	Bangfàng	Balmá (ban)	Bufáng.
Go	Tháng	....	Tháng-di.
Eat	Zá	Chá	Chá.
Come	Fai	Ibá	Fai.
Beat	Bu	Dak	Bu.
Die	Thoi	Tháng-zá	Thoi.
Behind	Unáu	....	Ulo (uno.)
Why	Mánŭ	Mánŭ	To-mána.
I	Áng	Áng-á	Áng.
Of me, mine	Áng-ni	Áng-ni	Á-ni.
To me	Áng-nŭ	Áng-ná	Á-na.
Me	Áng-khô	Áng-khô	(Ána ?)
We	Zang	Chingá	Chung.
Of us, our	Zang-ni	Ching-ni	Chi-ni.
You (thou)	Nang	Náá	Núng.
Of you (yours)	Nang-ni	Náng-ni	Ni-ni.
He	Bí	Uá	Bo.
Of him	Bí-ni	Uá-ni	Bi-ni.
A good man	Mànsŭí gahàm	Mándá námá	Borok káhám.
Of, &c., &c.	——— ni	——— ni	——— ni.
To, &c., &c.	——— nŭ	——— ná	——— na.
A bad boy	Sásè fisá hàmá	Shâksá bĭsá námjá.	Batsa hàmyá.

English.	*Kachári.*	*Gáro.*	*Hill Tipperá.*
I am ...	Áng dang-a.	....	Áng tong-o (ong).
Thou art ...	Nang dang-a.	....	Núng tong-o (ong).
He is ...	Bí dang-a.	....	Bo tong-o (ong).
We are ...	Zangfur dang-a.	....	Chung tong-o (ong).
You are ...	Nangsur dang-a.	....	Norok tong-o (ong).
They are ...	Bísur dang-a.	....	Borok tong-o (ong).
Beat ...	Bu ...	Dak ...	Bu.
To beat ...	Bu-nŭ ...	Dak-ná ...	Bu-nani.
Beating ...	Bu-ni (bu-ŭí)...	....	Bu-oi.
Having beaten	Bu-ná-noi ...	....	Bu-khá.
I, &c., beat ...	Áng, &c., bu-ĭŭ	....	Áng, &c., bu-yo.
I am beaten...	Áng bu-záï-ŭ ...	....	Áng bù ják-o.
I shall be beaten.	Áng bu-zá-gan	....	Áng bu já-kan-o.
I, &c., go ...	Áng tháng-ŭ ...	....	Áng, &c., tháng-yo.
Go ...	Tháng ...	....	Tháng-o.
Going ...	Tháng-ni (tháng-ŭí.)	....	Tháng oi.
What is your name?	Nang-ni náöá má?	Nang-ni mang mai?	Ni-ni mung to-má?
Give this rupee to him.	Bê thàkhá bí-nŭ hŭ.	Uá thánghá-kho uá-na án-bo.	Obana ba ráng ha rudi.
Walk before me	Áng-ni sĭgángáu thà-bai-láng.	Áng-ni mokháng há amih.	Á-ni sákángo him-di.
Whose boy comes behind you?	Nang-ni unáu sur-ni físá-zlá faidang?	Nang-ni jamáno sháo-ni bishá rebáengá?	Ni-ni uno sá-bá-ni batsa fai?
From whom did you buy (that)?	Nang sur-ni-frai (boi-khô) bai-nai?	Nang sá-onikho brebáhá?	Nang sábá-ni-tháni pai-kha?
From a shop-keeper of the village.	Gámi dukáni-ni-frai.	Cháng-ni du-káni-onikho.	Bári dukáni-tháni.
The boy (is) bad.	Físá zălá hàm-á	Bishá nám-já...	Chhá jalá hàm-yá.
Literally ...	Child-male good-not (is).	Child good-not (is.)	Child-male good-not (is).

A close examination of some of the phrases and sentences above given will show that the process of word-building is exactly alike in Kachári and Hill Tipperá. Thus, in both languages, the word for "boy" is really a *compound* word, "fĭsá" (K.) and "chhá" (H. T.), meaning simply a "child," while the following word, "zalá" (K.) or "jalá" (H. T.) is a kind of adjective,=masculine, male; so that the whole compound denotes in both languages alike, a "male child," a "boy." So again the word for "bad" is in both languages a negative term="not-good." The radical part of the word in each language is "hàm;" this root, with certain prefixes, "ga" (K.) and "ká" (H. T.), means "good;" but by dropping these prefixes, and attaching certain affixes—"á" (K.) and "yá" (H. T.)—we get an exactly opposite meaning, "good-not"=bad,—the method of word-building, and of making the same root express these opposite meanings, being exactly the same in both languages. It is highly probable that a closer study of the languages in use among the tribes inhabiting the hills to the south of the Surmá Valley, would reveal many other points of resemblance with the Kachári of the Brahmaputra Valley; so that there seems reason to believe that this form of non-Áryan speech (Kachári) was at one time, under slightly different forms, very widely used over the valley of Assam and the adjacent districts of North-East Bengal.—S. E.

TEZPUR, *the 12th June 1884.*

HILLS KACHARI COMPARED WITH THAT SPOKEN IN THE PLAINS.

FROM what is at present known—and our knowledge is scanty enough—it would seem that the Kachári language as spoken in North-East Bengal and the Kachári Duárs of the Goálpára, Kámrúp, and Darrang Districts in the Valley of Assam, is substantially the same as that in use in the North Kachár Hills,—at Gonjong, Maibong, Asálu, &c.

There are indeed many striking points of *difference;* and in some cases words in common use in everyday life (*e.g.*, man, woman, boy, goat, &c.) seem to have little or no etymological relation to each other as used respectively in the Valley and in the Hills. But on the whole, so far as the materials at present available for comparing the two forms of speech enable us to come to any definite conclusion as to the relation between them, it certainly seems that the points in which they *agree* far exceed both in number and importance those in which they *differ;* so that we shall probably not be far wrong in coming to the conclusion that the Kachári of the Hills and that of the Assam Valley are but different forms of what is at bottom essentially the same national language. A short Vocabulary, with some illustrations of the *inflections* in use in these two forms of speech, is given below, with a few typical sentences and some brief notes, &c.; and by carefully observing and weighing this list of words, sentences, &c., the student will be able at once to *compare* and to *contrast* the Kachári of the Plains with that spoken in the Hills, and thus form his own conclusion as to the relation existing between them.

I.—VOCABULARY.

English.	*Plains Kachári (Darrang).*	*Hills Kachári.*
One	... Sê	... Shê (si).
Two	... Nê (gnê)	... Gĭní (gní).
Three	... Thàm (găthàm)	... Găthàm (thàm).
Four	... Brŭí	... Birí.
Five	... Bá	... Bŭngá.
Six	... Ḍă (ṛă)	... Dă.
Seven	... Sní (sĭní)	... Siní.
Eight	... Zàt (jàt)	... Jái
Nine	... Skhó (sĭkhó)	... Shugú.
Ten	... Zi (ji)	... Ji.
I	... Áng	... Áng.
We	... Zang (jang)	... Jang (jing).
Thou	... Nang	... Nu (nung).
You	... Nang-sur	... Nu-shi (ni-shi).
He	... Bí	... Bwa.
They	... Bí-sur	... Bwa-nishi.
This	... Bê	... Eb.
These	... Bê-sur	... Eb-nishi.
That	... Boi	... Bwa.
Those	... Boi-sur	... Bwa-nishi.
Who	... Sur (sar)	... Shôr.
Rice (dhán)	... Mai	... Mai.
—— (chául)	... Mairang	... Mairang.
—— (bhát)	... Mikhàm	... Mákham.
Man	... Mànsŭí	... Shubung.
Woman	... Hingzháu	... Másháingjwu.
Child	... Fisá	... Ánchá.
House	... Nŭ	... Na.
Fire	... Åt	... Ôái.
Air	... Bàr	... Bár.
Earth	... Há	... Há.
Water	... Dŭí	... Dí.
Head	... Khârâ	... Khra.
Hair	... Khenai	... Khánai.
Eye	... Mêgan (mígan)	... Mu.

English.	*Plains Kachári.*	*Hills Kachári.*
Ear	... Khâmâ	... Kámáu.
Nose	... Gangthang	... Gung.
Mouth	... Khugá	... Mukháng.
Neck	... Gada	... Gada.
Hand	... Ákhai	... Iáu.
Body	... Mâdam	... Cháu.
Blood	... Thoi	... Twí.
Fish	... Ná (gná)	... Nwá.
Cow	... Mosaú	... Musu.
Goat	... Burmá	... Brúna.
Snake	... Zibaú (jibaú)	... Jhubu.
Bird	... Dáu	... Dáu.
Cock	... Dáu-zlá	... Dáu-na.
Hen	... Dáu-zu	... Dáu-má.
Egg	... Dáu-dŭí ("fowl's water.")	Dáu-dí ("fowl's water")
Tiger	... Mosá	... Misi.
Sheep	... Mendá	... Mená.
Earthquake	... Bánggri	... Bángglá.
Rain	... Nakhá (akhá)	... Hádi.
Mâdh (rice-beer)	... Zaú (jaú)	... Ju.
(To) eat	... Zá (já)	... Ji.
— drink	... Lang	... Lung.
— sleep	... Udu	... Thu.
— walk	... Thàbai	... Dáubai.
— run	... Khàt	... Khai.
— sit	... Zâ (jâ)	... Khám.
— laugh	... Mĭní (mní)	... Mĭní (mní).
— weep	... Gáb	... Grá.
— jump	... Bát	... Baitlum.
— come	... Fai	... Fai.
— go	... Tháng	... Tháng.
— cook	... Sang	... Sang.
— bring	... Lábo	... Lábu.
— take	... Láng	... Láng.
— give	... Hŭ	... Ri.
— give back	... Hŭ-fáfin	... Fini-ri.

II.—GRAMMAR (ACCIDENCE, INFLECTIONS, &c.)

1.—Nouns (declension).

Kachári. Plains.		Kachári. Hills.		English.
		SINGULAR.		
Nom.—Omá (omái-á)*	...	Hono	...	a pig.
Obj.—Omá-khô	...	Hono-khô	...	a pig.
Instr.—Omá-zang (jang)	...	Hono-jang	...	by (with) a pig.
Dat.—Omá-nŭ	...	Hono-ne	...	to „
Abl.—Omá-ni-frai	...	Hono-ni-frang	...	from „
Poss.—Omá-ni	...	Hono-ni	...	of „
Loc.—Omái-áu	...	Hono-há	...	in „
Voc.—Heloi omá!	...	Hoko-hono!	...	O pig!
		PLURAL.		
Nom.—Omá-fŭr (far; frá)	...	Hono-ráu	...	pigs.
Obj.—Omá-fŭr-khô	...	Hono-ráu-khô	...	pigs.
&c. &c.		&c. &c.		

The remaining case-endings in both forms of the language (Hills and Plains) are exactly the same as those given above for the Singular number.

2.—Verbs (conjugation, &c.)

(*a*).—*Simple Verb Active.*

Verbal root, "Nu" (nai), to see.

English.		*Plains Kachári.*		*Hills Kachári.*
I see	...	Áng nuĭ-ŭ*	...	Áng nai-re.
I am seeing	...	Áng nu-dang	...	Áng nu-du.
I saw	...	Áng nu-bai	...	Áng nai-bá.
I did see	...	Áng { nu-nai / nu-dang-man	...	Áng { nu-bá. / nu-khá.
I shall see	...	Áng nu-gan	...	Áng nai-náng.
See thou (you)	...	Nu	...	Nai.
Let him see	...	Nu-thang	...	Ba-ne pu-nu.

* This second form of the word (omái-á), is the nominative *emphatic* or *definite.*—See Grammar, page 11. D. The letter "i" is *euphonically* affixed to the second syllable in the nominative definite and locative cases; as also to the verbal root in the present indefinite tense ("nu-ĭ-ŭ;" "záa-ĭ-ŭ," &c).

English.	*Plains Kachári.*	*Hills Kachári.*
I can see ...	Áng nu-nŭ há-gaú ...	Áng nai pure.
I could see ...	Áng nu-nŭ há-bai ...	Áng nai pure-mu.
If I see ...	Áng {nu-bá / nu-blá} ...	Jadi áng nu-re.
If I saw ...	Áng {nu-bá / nu-blá} ...	Jadi áng nu-káde.
Seeing ...	Nuï ...	Nuhi.
Having seen ...	Nu-nánoi ...	Nuhi-dádá.
To see ...	Nu-nŭ ...	Nuhi-má.

(*b*).—*Passive Voice* (*used sparingly in both forms of speech*).

I am seen ...	Áng nunai záaï-ŭ ...	Áng nu jáu-du.
I was seen ...	Áng nunai záa-bai ...	Áng nu jáu-khá.
I shall be seen ...	Áng nunai záa-gan ...	Áng nu jáu-náng.
I can be seen ...	———— záa-nŭ há-gaú.	Áng nu jáu pure.
I could be seen ...	Áng nunai záa-nŭ há-bai	Áng nu jáu pure-mu.
If I am seen ...	Áng nunai záa-bá ...	Jadi áng nu jáu-re.

(*c*)—*Negative Verb.*

I see not ...	Áng nu-á ...	Áng nai-á.
I saw not ...	Áng nu-á-khŭí ...	Áng nai-á-bá.
I shall not see ...	Áng nu-á ...	Áng nai-á-náng.
See not ...	Dá nu ...	Dá nai.
Let him not see ...	Dá nu-thang ...	Ba-khô dá pu-nu.

(*d*)—*Causative Verb.*

I show ...	Áng nu-hŭï-ŭ ...	Áng pu-nu.
I showed ...	Áng nu-hŭ-bai ...	Áng pu-nu-{bá. / khá.}
I shall show ...	Áng nu-hŭ-gan ...	Áng pu-nu-náng.
Let him show ...	Bí nu-hŭ-thang ...	Ba-khô pu-numá-ri.
I can show ...	Áng nu-hŭ-nŭ há-gaú	Áng pu-nu pure.
I could show ...	Áng nu-hŭ-nŭ há-bai ...	Áng pu-nu pure-mu.
If I show ...	Áng nu-hŭ-bá ...	Jadi áng pu-nu-re.

3.—Illustrative Sentences, with Literal Translation given underneath each Sentence.

English.	*Plains Kachári.*	*Hills Kachári.*
1.—I will give you six annas each.	Áng sá-fá sá-fá-nŭ áná-ṛâ hŭ-gan I man by (to) man annas-six give-will	Áng sáu-si sáu-si-ne áná-ḍa ri-náng. I man by (to) man annas-six give-will.
2.—I saw three men, four cows, and five tigers.	Áng mànsŭí sá-thàm, mosaú má-brŭí, áru mosá má-bá nu-bai. I men three, cows four, and tigers five see-did.	Áng shubung má-găthàm, musu má-birí, dába misi má-bungá nu-bá. I men three, cows four, and tigers five see-did.
3.—The elephant is bigger than the tiger.	Mosá-nŭ-khri háthi-á gădat′... Tiger-than elephant-the great (is)	Misi-thá míŭng ded-áu. Tiger-than elephant great-is.
4.—Did you bring the cow yesterday?	Míá nang mosaú-khô lábo-bai ná? Yesterday you cow (*obj.*) bring-did?	Míáhá nung musu lábu-bá? Yesterday you cow bring-did?
5.—Kacháris drink mâdh ...	Bâṛâ-fisá zaú lang-ú... Kacháris mâdh drink-(habitually) ...	Dímáshá-ráu ju lung-re. Kacháris mâdh drink-(habitually).
6.—That man is (now) drinking mâdh.	Boi mànsŭí zaú lang-dang ... That man mâdh drinking-is ...	Hôëb shubung ju lung-du. That man mâdh drinking-is.
7.—I shot at the tiger and killed it.	Áng mosá-khô gáu-thàt-bai ... I tiger (*obj.*) shoot-kill-did ...	Áng misi-khô gáu-thai-bá. I tiger (*obj.*) shoot-kill-did.
8.—He says he will not go to-day.	Bí khĭthăĭ-ŭ díni tháng-á ... He says, to-day (I) go-not ...	Bwa thi-re díni tháng-i-á. He says, to-day (I) go-not.
9.—I will come, if I can ...	Há-bá, áng fai-gan ... Can-if, I come-will ...	Blai-káde, áng fai-náng. Can-if, I come-will.
10.—I would have come, if I could.	Há-blá, áng fai-gaú-man ... Could-if, I come-would-have ...	Blai-káde, áng fai-khá-mu. Could if, I come-would-have.

I.—VOCABULARY.

A glance at the list of words given above will show that by far the greater part of them obviously stand in very close etymological relation to each other. There are indeed some remarkable exceptions to this rule; *e.g.*, the words for man, woman, child, goat, body, &c., seem to be quite distinct, and as these must be words in common, every-day use in village life, we might have expected beforehand to have found a greater likeness, if not identity, existing in the use of these terms. But however these differences may be accounted for, there can be no doubt that the words for the numerals up to ten, the personal pronouns, &c., are substantially the same; and this statement holds good of the great majority of the words given in the Vocabulary.

II.—GRAMMAR.

1.—Accidence.

Nouns.

The inflection, &c., of nouns has clearly very much in common in both forms of speech. Gender is usually denoted, not by entirely different words (*e.g.*, boy, girl, &c.), but by using an indeterminate word (child), and appending to it some qualifying term; *e.g.*,—

P. K.*—"Fĭsá" (fsá), child { "fĭsá zălá," child-male = boy. / "fĭsá zu," child-female = girl.

H. K.*—"Ánchá," child { "ánchá bámá," child-male = boy. / "ánchá bachhu," child-female = girl.

In expressing the *number* of nouns, there is a marked difference between the two forms of speech. The only plural

* P. K. attached to a word or phrase denotes the *Plains* Kachári equivalent for that word or phrase, whilst H. K. indicates the forms used by the *Hills* Kacháris.

termination in common use in the Plains, is "fŭr" (far, frá). This seems to be quite unknown in the Hills, where plurality is usually expressed by "ráu" (ráo), or "nishi,"—forms which are never heard among the Kacháris of Darrang. It is difficult to account for this marked difference in the plural termination of nouns: it is just possible that the Hill Kacháris may have borrowed the former (ráu) of the two plural terminations above-given from the Bengáli (erá, rá), while the latter may have been adopted from some neighbouring hill-tribe.

As regards the *case-endings*, a very striking resemblance does undoubtedly exist between the two forms of speech. Thus, the methods of denoting the Objective, Instrumental, and Possessive cases are absolutely identical, whilst the case-endings for the Dative, Ablative, and Locative inflections have obviously very much in common. In the mode of inflecting the noun then, it may fairly be assumed that the two forms of speech are substantially the same.

Verbs.

In the method of conjugating the verb, some striking points of resemblance present themselves, which hardly admit of being explained away as mere accidental coincidences. Thus in both modes of speech the present tense has two forms, a present indefinite and a present definite, *e.g.*,—

P. K.—"Áng mikhàm záī-ŭ,"* } I eat rice, *i.e.*, at *any* time,
H. K.—"Áng mákham ji-re," } habitually.
P. K.—"Áng mikhàm zá-dang," } I am eating rice, *i.e.*, now,
H. K.—"Áng mákham ji-du," } at this very moment.

The *Passive Voice* is expressed in the usual way in both forms of speech, *i.e.*, by combining the past participle of the principal verb with the various tenses of the verb "be, become." It will be observed that the verbal root to denote the substantive verb (be, become) is etymologically the same, *i.e.*, P. K.,

* "Záī-ŭ,"—"ī" inserted *euphonically* between root (zá) and temporal affix (ŭ.)

"záa," (jáa); H. K., "jáu." Among the Kacháris of the Hills and of the Plains alike the Passive Voice is used very sparingly and unfrequently, as indeed is the case in other Oriental languages (*e.g.*, Hindustáni, Assamese, &c.)

Negative Verb.

A negative force is given to the verb—*not* in the way common to many languages, *i.e.*, by *prefixing* some adverb of negation (non, ne, not, &c.), but by *affixing* a letter or syllable to the verbal stem. In both forms of speech the affix used for that purpose is "á" in the present tense [P. K., "Nu-á;" H. K., "Nai-á," (I) see not], while the past tenses are expressed by an additional affix in accordance with the same principle. But in the Imperative Mood this principle is departed from, both forms of speech agreeing in expressing the prohibitory negative, not by an *affix*, but by a *prefix*, "dá;" P. K., "Dá nu;" H. K., "Dá nai,"=see not; look not. A strictly analogous mode of giving a negative force to the verbal root prevails in the Gáro and Mikir languages, as well as in that of Hill Tipperá (see Grammar, pp. 23-24).

Causative Verb.

In Hills Kachári a causal force is given to the verbal root by the prefix, "pu;" *e.g.*, "Nu-má," to see; "Pu-nu-má," to cause to see, to show. The Kacháris of the Plains usually express the same meaning in a somewhat different way, *i.e.*, by appending to the verbal root a second verb, "hŭ-nŭ," to give; thus (P. K.) "Nu-hŭ-nŭ," to give (*i.e.*, to cause) to see, to show. But some verbs acquire a causal force much in the same way with verbal roots among the Hills Kacháris, *i.e.*, by *prefixing* a syllable, *e.g.*, "fă" (fĭ). Thus (P. K.), "Ràn-nŭ," to be dry; "fă-ràn-nŭ," to cause to be dry, to dry (active); "sí-nŭ," to be wet; "fĭ-sí-nŭ," to cause to be wet, to steep, soak (see Grammar, page 25.B). With this may be compared the analogous usage prevailing in the Mikir language, where a causal sense is given to a word by the prefix "pè," *e.g.*, "mésén," good (*adj.*), "pè-mésén," to cause to be good, to make good.

2.—Syntax (sentences.)

The conclusion, to which a cursory inspection of the Vocabulary and Accidence above given would apparently lead us (*i.e.*, that the two forms of speech are substantially the same language), is certainly borne out by what we know of the *Syntax* in each case. Ten typical sentences are given above, with a literal and verbal translation appended to each; and a glance at these will at once show how much the two forms of speech have in common as regards the syntactical relation of words. The *order* of the words is almost absolutely the same in either case, and much the same may be said of the process of word-building and the syntactical combination of words and phrases in sentences. Many of the characteristic features of the Kachári (Plains) language have their exact counterparts in the speech of the Kacháris of the Hills. Thus when more than one object is spoken of, the numeral almost invariably *follows* the noun it refers to, this numeral itself being preceded by a classifying particle, usually monosyllabic. (See Grammar, page 13). Exactly the same usage obtains in Hill Kachári, as well as in Gáro and other cognate languages. Thus in sentences 1 and 2, "áná-ṛå" (P. K.) and "áná-ḍå" (H. K.)=annas-six (six annas); "mànsŭí sá-thàm" (P. K.), "shubung má-găthàm" (H. K.)=men-three; "mosaú má-brŭí" (P. K.), "musu má-birí" (H. K.)=cows-four, &c. &c. In sentences 5 and 6, we have the two forms of the present tense, indefinite and definite, above referred to: "lang-ŭ" (drink) and "lang-dang" (is drinking) (P. K.) exactly corresponding to "lung-re" and "lung-du" (H. K.). (See Grammar, pages 17, 19). In sentence 7 another marked feature common to both forms of speech is brought out; *i.e.*, the way in which two verbal roots are combined into a compound verb, the *second* root in such compounds indicating the *result* of the whole action denoted by the compound verb, whilst the former root shows the *manner* in which this result was attained. (See Grammar, page 27). Thus, "gáu-nŭ," to shoot, combined with "thàṭ-nŭ," to kill (P. K.),=to shoot to death. Exactly the same meaning is conveyed in almost exactly the same way in Hill Kachári, the second root undergoing a slight change; "thàṭ" (P. K.)="thai" (H. K.); "gáu-thai-bá" (H. K.)="gáu-tháṭ-bai" (P. K.), shot and killed. In sentence 8, we find in both forms of speech alike the *present* tense of the Negative Verb taking the same form as the future; "tháng-á" (P. K.) and "tháng-i-á" (H. K.), "go not," being used in the sense of "will not go." In sentences 9 and 10 the method of expressing contingency, &c. (subjunctive mood) is seen to be the same in both forms of speech in *principle*, *i.e.*, by an *affix*, not by a *prefixed* word; though the exact *form* taken by this affix differs largely, *e.g.*, "bá" (blá) (P. K.)="káde" (H. K.): "há-bá" (P. K.)="blai-káde" (H. K.), can-if, *i.e.*, if (I) can. Sometimes both forms of speech in expressing contingency fall back upon a *prefixed* word, "jadi" (if)—a term evidently borrowed from their Hindu (Bengáli or Assamese) surroundings; but the more common method, at least in the Plains, is that given above (by the affix "bá" or "blá"), equivalent to the H. K. "káde;" and here though the affixes differ in *form*, yet the *principle* which underlies and governs their application is obviously one and the same.

On the whole, then, a review of the Vocabulary, and certain leading features of the Accidence and Syntax of the Kachári language as spoken in the Hills and Plains respectively, leads naturally to the conclusion that the two forms of speech are at bottom substantially the same. As before pointed out, there are some difficultios attending this theory, *i.e.*, the entirely different words used to express certain familiar ideas that must be in every-day use, *e.g.*, the words for man, woman, boy, goat, &c.; but the points in which the two forms of speech *agree* very much exceed, both in number and in importance, those in which they *differ*; and we may perhaps fairly infer that the Kacháris of the Hills and those of the Plains, though they use different national names (Bårạ̊ and Dímáshá), and can only partially understand each other's speech, are essentially one and the same people. What was the original home of this people, it is not at all easy to say. Their features are often of a distinctively Mongolian type, and with their almond-shaped eyes, projecting cheek-bones, and scanty beard, they sometimes show a certain approximation to the Chinese type of face,—a fact that would seem to point to the countries to the North-East of Assam as their original dwelling-place. As stated elsewhere, some of the various names by which they are known (Hojai, Hájong, Dímáshá) point to a land of mountains and rivers as their natural home; and perhaps we shall not be far wrong (though this is little better than guess-work) if we look upon the hills around the upper course of the Subansíri, Díhong, and Díbong rivers as the primal dwelling-place of the Kachári race. Descending from these hills, they may for a time have occupied the upper portion of the Assam Valley, where the names of the principal rivers (Dí-bru, Dí-hing, Dí-sáng, Dí-khu, Dí-hong, Dí-bong, Dí-krang) still begin with what is perhaps meant to be the Kachári word for water (dŭí, dí), and where a non-Áryan tribe (the Deori Chutiás) still speak a language said to be closely related to the Kachári tongue. Under pressure, perhaps, from invading tribes from the North-East (Áhoms, Mattacks, &c.), they gradually made their way westwards to the neighbourhood of the Dhansíri river, where they would appear to have separated into two distinct branches. One of these branches made its way up the Dhansíri Valley to Dŭímá-pur (*i.e.*, "Big-river-town"), where a powerful Kachári community existed for some years; and thence over the North Kachár Hills *viâ* Asálu, Maibong, &c., into the Surmá Valley, and even beyond it to some of the hills which form its southern boundary, *e.g.*, Hill Tipperá, the language of which has undoubtedly much in common with the Kachári of the Plains. The other branch would seem to have crossed the Brahmaputra, and gradually to have occupied the whole of the sub-montane tract bordering the southern frontier of Bhután, from the neighbourhood of Tezpur to that of Jalpaiguri and Dárjíling—a region varying from ten to thirty miles in breadth, where the bulk of the population is still Kachári (Båṛå), and where, in spite of outside Hindu influence, they to a great extent still retain their national language, religion, and customs, &c., unchanged. Large numbers of them have indeed been Hinduized, and under various names (Kôch, Rájbansis, &c.,) are often loosely classified as Hindus, though their features, &c., speak unmistakeably of a non-Áryan origin; and as such they form numerically one of the most powerful constituent elements in the population of this province. No less an authority than Mr. Brian Hodgson has said that the great bulk of the population of thé Assam Valley is of non-Áryan origin; and to this element in the population the people vaguely known to us as Kacháris have no doubt *very* largely contributed.

But whatever their origin, or their past history, may have been, there can be little doubt that they have a future before them of some promise. Intellectually inferior to their Hindu and Massalmán neighbours, they are physically and morally vastly their superiors. Their liberal diet—for they eat freely every kind of flesh, that of the cow alone excepted—tends to give them a sturdy physique,—a result to which their industrious habits also largely contribute; whilst in their simplicity, straightforwardness, and freedom from crooked, deceitful ways, they give proof of a type of character which one often looks for in vain among more "civilized" communities. Hitherto, they have been little more than "hewers of wood and drawers of water,"—essentially a people supporting themselves by unskilled manual labour. But now that education is spreading among them, they are gradually forcing their way to higher things. Several old pupils of the Kachári Mission Schools in Darrang now fill positions of importance and responsibility as mouzádárs, mandals, &c., while others act as mohurirs in tea-factories, and have virtual charge of these factories during the absence of the European managers. There is reason, then, to hope that the Kachári element in the population of this province will come to the front more and more; and play an increasingly important part in raising themselves and their neighbours to higher and better things.

S. ENDLE.

SHILLONG, *the 18th July, 1884.*

The compiler gladly takes this opportunity of acknowledging his many and great obligations to the officer in charge of the North Kachár Hills, Mr. Soppitt, without whose co-operation, most freely and repeatedly given at the cost of much time and labour, the foregoing sketch comparing the Kachári of the Plains with that of the Hills, could not possibly have been drawn up at all. It may be hoped that this officer may see his way towards publishing an Outline Grammar of the language of the North Kachár Hills—a work the satisfactory carrying out of which is the more to be desired, as the Hill Kacháris have been less exposed to Hindu and other outside influences than their fellow-countrymen in the Plains have been, and among them, therefore, we may reasonably expect to find the national mother-tongue preserved in its purest form.—S. E.

OUTLINE KACHÁRI GRAMMAR.

ABBREVIATIONS.

Most of the abbreviations made use of will explain themselves, being merely shortened forms of the words they represent. The following may however be noted:—

Cf.—(confer) compare.

Lit.—Literally.

Adj.—Adjective.

Part.—Participle.

A., *H.*—These letters indicate respectively the Assamese and Hindustáni equivalents of certain Kachári words and phrases to which they are appended in brackets. These are given to assist the learner in passing "from the known to the unknown," it being taken for granted that Magistrates, Planters, and others, to whom a knowledge of Kachári is likely to be useful, are already familiar with the Assamese and Hindustáni languages.

OUTLINE KACHARI GRAMMAR.

THE following sketch of some of the leading features and principles of the Kachári language is comprised under three heads—I. Orthography, II. Accidence, and III. Syntax. This last-mentioned subject is perhaps, in a language of this character never yet reduced to writing, best taught by means of typical sentences, which serve at once to illustrate the accidence and the syntactical relation of words, explanatory remarks being inserted wherever called for.

PART I.—ORTHOGRAPHY.

In attempting to represent the sounds of this language by means of written symbols, it must be understood that nothing further than approximate correctness is aimed at. The consonants, indeed, present little difficulty, most of them being pronounced much as they are in English. But some of the vowel sounds are peculiar, and (as might be expected in an unwritten tongue) the pronunciation of these is not always uniform, though the divergence of sounds is less than might have been anticipated. The student cannot be too strongly urged to study the different sounds of the language as they fall from the lips of the people themselves. He should particularly endeavour to master the distinction between the various modifications of the different *vowel* sounds, as these sometimes indicate very important differences in meaning; *e.g.*—

"Bè sŭímá {âṛŭ" / âṛá"} This dog {bites. / does not bite.

Here the distinction between the two vowel sounds "ŭ" and "á" indicates all the wide difference between an affirmative and a negative proposition.

1.—VOWELS.

a—unaccented, always short, as in "comp*a*ny," "Americ*a*"; *e.g.*, "Ban," firewood. This sound is somewhat more abrupt and explosive than in English, especially when *final*.

á—long, as in "f*a*ther"; *e.g.*, "Tháng," go. This sound is sometimes drawn out and prolonged,—a modification which may be represented by "áa"; *e.g.*—

"Zá-nŭ," to eat.
"Záa-nŭ," to be, become.

à—sharp, short sound, as in "p*a*n"; *e.g.*, "Gădàn," new.

å—broad sound, as in "c*a*ll," or like "o" in "*o*rder," "f*o*r"; *e.g.*, "Gåthå," a child.

e—unaccented, as in "b*e*d," "th*e*n"; *e.g.*, "Gădet," great.

ê—as "*ey*" in "th*ey*"; *e.g.*, "Mêgan," eye.

è—an intermediate sound between the two former; *e.g.*, "Bèsè," how many? how much?

i—unmarked, short, as in "p*i*n"; *e.g.*, "Ling," call.

í—long, as in "mar*i*ne"; *e.g.*, "Bí," he.

o—unmarked, short, as in "st*o*p"; *e.g.*, "Mosá," a tiger.

ô—long, as in "b*o*ne"; *e.g.*, "Khô" (sign of objective case).

This sound "ô" is occasionally thickened and strengthened so as to approximate to the sound of "aú" (see below), with which indeed it seems at times to be interchangeable. In such cases what seems to be the more correct sound is given first, the less usual sound being represented by appending "aú" in parentheses; *e.g.*, "Khô" (khaú).

u—short, as in "p*u*ll."

ú—long, as in "p*oo*l"; *e.g.*, "Búnŭ," to beat.

ŭ*—This is a sound difficult to describe. It bears some resemblance to the (å) given above, but is much more compressed. In uttering it the cheeks are drawn in close to the jaws, the lips but slightly apart, and the tongue placed near the outer edge of the hard palate, the breath being allowed to escape slowly between the two latter organs with a semi-nasal intonation. At the end of a word this sound has something in common with the *bisarga* in Bengáli ; *e.g.*, "Bŭnŭ," to drag, pull.

au—as "*ow*" in "*how*"; *e.g.*, "Gălau," long.

aú—approximates to ô ; *e.g.*, "Găthaú," deep. (See "ô" above).

áu—in uttering this diphthong the voice dwells on the "á" sound, the unaccented "u" serving merely to modify the whole sound in the direction of "ow"; *e.g.*, "Gakháu," bitter. The distinction between these two sounds, which it is not always easy for the ear to catch, is sometimes of practical importance ; *e.g.*—

"Bê dŭí-á {găthaú / gătháu} ná?" Is this water {deep? / sweet?

ai, as "i" in "wine," "shine"; *e.g.*, "Mai," rice (paddy).

ŭí—this is a peculiar sound, which seems to fluctuate between "oi" (pronounced *very short*) and "í." It is apparently made up of the "ŭ" sound above described and "í," the voice gliding rapidly over the former vowel and dwelling on the latter, the whole sound approximating to "í." Occasionally the sounds of both vowels are *separately* heard, though not perhaps with such distinctness as to call for the use of the diœresis ; *e.g.*, "Dŭímá," a river ; "Sŭímá," a dog.

oi, as "oi" in "boil"; *e.g.*, "Thoinŭ," to die.

---

* The sound intended to be denoted by this symbol would be more correctly represented by *short o*, but this character was not available at the Secretariat Press.

2.—CONSONANTS.

Most of these, as before stated, are used as in English, and call for no particular description. But some are used to represent peculiar sounds or modifications of familiar sounds, and to designate these certain diacritical marks are necessary.

c—not used; its soft sound being represented by "s," its hard sound by "k." The combinations "ch" and "chh" seem to be unknown in Kachári.

d, dh } ḍ, ḍh } These letters are used much as in Assamese, the two former letters being properly dental sounds, the two latter, cerebral. Cerebral sounds seem to predominate in the language, dental letters being used chiefly in words borrowed from the Sanscrit family; *e.g.*, "Dharam" (dharmma); and even in these cases the Kacháris generally substitute a cerebral sound for a dental one, the distinction between dental and cerebral letters being but rarely observed. The cerebral "ḍ" and "ṭ" sometimes pass into "ṛ"; thus, the name by which Kacháris speak of themselves may be written indifferently "Bâṛâ" or "Bâḍâ."

f—as in English, but strongly aspirated, especially at the beginning of a word.

g—always hard, as in "*gun*"; *e.g.*, "Gălau," long.

h—as in English (simple aspirate); *e.g.*, "Hŭnŭ," to give. Sometimes this becomes a *guttural* aspirate, the two sounds being apparently interchangeable, and used without any obvious difference of meaning.

n̲—this is the nasal sound (rare in Kachári) found in the Hindustani "men̲," &c.; in French, "l'*en*fa*n*t," &c.

ng—this combination is very rarely found at the beginning of a word in Kachári, but is not uncommon at the end of a word or syllable, in which case it is pronounced exactly like the "ng" in "si*ng*i*ng*": *e.g.*, "Á*ng*," I; "Thá*ng*," go. In these cases the "g" sound always combines with the preceding nasal, and is not carried on to the next syllable; *e.g.*, "Thá*ng*-á," (I) will not go.

The nasal sounds (*anunásika*) so common in Assamese, represented by the *chandra-bindu* (̐), seem not to be found in Kachári.

p—as in English.

ph—an aspirated p, something like the English "ph" in "u*ph*old," the sounds of the two letters, however, being not heard separately as in the English word, but combining into a single sound.

r—with a broader, more rolling sound than in English.

ṛ—sometimes interchanges with "ṭ" and "ḍ"; *e.g.*—

"Bí kháṭdang," he is running.
"Bí kháṛá," he does not run.

s—as in "this"; *e.g.*, "Fĭsá," a son child: often with a sharp semi-aspirated sound, especially when *initial.*

t, th} ṭ, ṭh} pronounced much as in Assamese, dental and cerebral, though this distinction often seems not to be strictly observed. The English sounds of "th" in "*th*is" and "*th*ing" are not found in Kachári.

v, w, y—as in English, the two latter always retaining their consonantal sound.

z—as in English; *e.g.*, "Zánŭ," to eat.

zh—like the French "j" in "*j*oli": *e.g.*, "Hing*zh*áusá," a woman.

In writing words borrowed from other languages (*e.g.*, Assamese) the Kacháris often change an unaspirated initial consonant into an aspirated one: thus, "Kál" (time) becomes "khál"; "Kintu" (but), "khintu," &c.

3.—ACCENTS: THE DIŒRESIS, &c.

In order to give some idea of the cadence of the language, two accents are made use of, the single and the double.

The single accent is used in short words, and is written in the form commonly called the acute accent (′); *e.g.*, "Tháng′nŭ," to go.

In longer words we sometimes have two accented syllables; *e.g.*, in the English word "in′deter″minate," the main accent (″) lies on the third syllable, while at the same time a certain stress is laid on the first syllable, the voice seeming to rest on it to gain strength for the utterance of a long word. In such cases the main, or principal, accent is represented by the double mark (″), the secondary one by the single sign (′). Thus the above word is written, "in′deter″minate." This system is used in representing the cadence of Kachári words of several syllables: *e.g.*, "Tháng′-ni-áu″-nŭ" (even while going), a participle from the root "Tháng" (go) above given. Here the last syllable, "nŭ," is a kind of enclitic; the main accent falling on the third syllable, and the secondary one on the first.

The diœresis is sometimes used over vowels to mark the beginning of a new syllable; *e.g.*—

"Guru′ï" (=gu-ru′-i), soft.

The hyphen is occasionally used in cases where confusion or doubt might arise from its absence; as, "Nŭ-áu," in a house.

As it is undesirable to multiply diacritical marks needlessly, such symbols as the diœresis, hyphen, &c., are used only very sparingly, and each diphthong and vowel must be supposed to have its full phonetic value, even when not separated by the hyphen, &c.: *e.g.*, "Oá" (bamboo) might be otherwise written "owá," "oyá," "o-á," &c.; so, "Faiá" (comes not) might be written "fai-á," &c. No consonant is ever needlessly doubled, and every such letter must be allowed its full force; *e.g.*, "Thánggan" (will go)="tháng-gan," &c.

The symbol (˘) over a letter denotes that it is to be pronounced as *shortly* as possible. It is used especially in the case of adjectives, many of which begin with the syllable "Gă": *e.g.*, "Găzá'," red; "Găfút'," white, &c. Here the first syllable is *very* short, and the words might almost be written, "gzá," "gfút," &c., the vowel in the first syllable being omitted altogether.

General Rules relating to Accent, &c.

1.—The accented syllable is indicated by the acute (′).

2.—In words where no syllabic accent is used the stress of the voice always rests on the *first* syllable of a word; *e.g.*, "Faidang" = "fai'dang"; "Faidangman" = "fai'dangman," &c.

This rule holds good even in words where the second (or later) syllable of a word contains a long vowel whilst the first syllable has only a short one, accent being to some extent independent of the *quantity* of vowel sounds; *e.g.*, "Mosá" (tiger) = "mo'sá," &c.

Exception.—In adjectives beginning with "gă" the *second* syllable is almost always the accented one; *e.g.*, "Găzá" (red) = "găzá'."

3.—In words of more than two syllables the accent, as a general rule, rests on the last syllable but one (penultimate).

4.—Nouns in declension—

A noun which in its simplest form takes the accent on its *first* syllable sometimes transfers it to its *second* when the case endings are appended; *e.g.*, "Mo'sá," a tiger; "Mosá'ni," of a tiger, &c.

5.—Verbs for the most part retain their original accent (first syllable) throughout their conjugation; but in compound verbs, the *second* member of the compound usually takes the accent; *e.g.*—

"Gorai-á { khàṭ′-bai," / khàṭ-láng′-bai," } The horse { ran. / ran away.

In verbal roots of more than one syllable, the accent almost always falls on the *second* syllable: *e.g.*, "Ga-glai-nŭ" (to fall) = "ga-glai′-nŭ"; "ge-le-nŭ" (to play) = "ge-le′-nŭ," &c.

Enclitics—"nŭ," (no,) "sŭí," ("soí,")—cause the accent to rest on the syllable immediately preceding them; *e.g.*—

"Bí { ga-glai′-nai" / ga-glai-nai′-sŭí" } he fell.

N.B.—A certain licence seems to be allowed in the spelling and pronouncing of some words. Thus, the word for "great," in its usual form "Gadat′," may be written and pronounced, "Gădad′," "Găded′," "Gădet′," "Gădit′," "Gădíd′," &c.; while in relation to other words, *e.g*, when in the superlative degree or when combined with a verb, the first syllable may be suppressed altogether; as—

"Boinŭsári detsiná" (for "Gădet′siná"), the greatest of all.

PART II.—ACCIDENCE.

In dealing with the accidence of the Kachári language, it will be convenient to speak of it under six heads:—1, Nouns; 2, Adjectives; 3, Pronouns; 4, Verbs; 5, Adverbs; and 6, other indeclinable words,—Prepositions, Conjunctions, and Interjections.

I.—NOUNS.

1.—GENDER.

A.—Nouns denoting inanimate objects have no formal distinction of gender, as, "Nŭ," a house; "Mai," rice (paddy).

B.—Nouns denoting animate objects have their gender distinguished by a qualifying word placed *after* the noun whose gender it indicates. These words vary as applied to distinct classes of objects. Some of those in common use are the following:—

(*a*) "Hôá," man (male); "Hingzháu," woman (female). These words are applied exclusively to human beings.

(*b*) Goats, deer, &c.—"Fànthá," "fànthi," are the terms used; *e.g.*, stag, "Mâí fànthá"; hind, "Mâí fànthi."

(*c*) Hogs, &c.—"Búndá," "búndi."
Boar, "Omá búndá"; sow, "Omá búndi."

(*d*) Birds, &c.—"Zălá," "zŭ."
Cock, "Dáu zălá"; hen, "Dáu zŭ."

(*e*) Elephants.—"Mákhúndá," "mákhúndi," &c.

Of these qualifying words indicating gender, it will be observed that—

(*a*) They generally, if not invariably, follow the word they qualify; and

(*b*) The final vowel is "á" when they denote the masculine gender, and "í" when they designate the feminine.

2.—Number.

Only two numbers are recognised, Singular and Plural.

The Singular is indicated simply by the name of the object; as, "Mànsŭí," a man. This is sometimes made more emphatic by the addition of a word meaning one; *e.g.*, "Mànsŭí sásè faibai," *one* man (and one only) came.

The Plural is denoted by the termination "fur," for which the syllables "frá" and "far" are sometimes substituted, especially in the oblique cases, without any obvious difference of meaning, *e.g.*:—

"Mànsŭí," a man. "Mànsŭí-fur," men.
"Nŭ," a house. "Nŭ-fur," houses.

The plural termination seems to be but rarely omitted, even in the case of nouns denoting inanimate objects.

3.—Case.

The following form gives the various case-endings, which are applicable alike to all nouns and pronouns. For the sake of convenience, the noun in Kachári is regarded as having eight cases, after the model of the noun in the Sanscrit family of languages; *i.e.*, Nominative, Objective, Instrumental, Dative, Ablative, Possessive, Locative, and Vocative :—

	Singular.			*Plural.*		
Nom.	Mànsŭí	... a		Mànsŭífur-(far)	...	
Obj.	Mànsŭí-khô (khaú)	... a		Mànsŭífur-khô (khaú)		
Instr.	Mànsŭí-zang	... by		Mànsŭífur-zang	... by	
Dat.	Mànsŭí-nŭ	... to		Mànsŭífur-nŭ	... to	
Abl.	Mànsŭí-ni-frai	...from	a man.	Mànsŭífur-ni-frai	...from	men.
Poss.	Mànsŭí-ni	... of		Mànsŭífur-ni	... of	
	Mànsŭí-há	... of		Mànsŭífur-há	... of	
Loc.	Mànsŭí-(ni)-áu	... in		Mànsŭífur-ni-áu	... in	
Voc.	Helŭí mànsŭí	... O		Helŭí mànsŭífur	... O	

A.—The Possessive case has two signs, "ni" and "há." Of these the former is by far the more frequently used, the latter being restricted chiefly to nouns denoting animate life.

B.—The Ablative case takes before its own termination, "frai," that of the Possessive case, "ni"; "Ni-frai"=from (out) of, &c.

C.—This holds good in some instances, though not in all, of the Locative case, "ní-áu." Sometimes when the Nominative case ends in a vowel "a" or "á," the case-ending of the Locative is preceded by "i" forming a diphthong with the preceding vowel; *e.g.*, "Nŭ + í + áu," = "Nŭí-áu," in a house. Thus the Locative case of "Nŭ," a house, may be written in three ways,—1, "Nŭ-áu"; 2, "Nŭi-áu"; 3, "Nŭ-ni-áu." The choice in the use of one or other of these forms seems to be determined largely by considerations of euphony and facility of utterance.

D.—When the Nominative case ends in the vowel "a" or "á," an affix (á) is often appended to it in composition when it forms the subject of a sentence: the final vowel of the Nominative being then strengthened by the addition of the vowel "i," with which it forms the diphthong "ai" (see note C). In such cases the affix (á) seems to have something of the force of the definite article; *e.g.*, "Dáu zălá găsípdang," a cock is crowing; "Dáu zăláí-á găsípdang," *the* cock (*i.e.*, the one I am now listening to) is crowing.

II.—ADJECTIVES.

4.—The adjective in Kachári is placed sometimes before, sometimes after, the noun it qualifies, without any very obvious difference of meaning, as—

"Găhàm mànsŭí-khô } nubai," I saw a good man.
"Mànsŭí găhàm-khô }

From the sentence above given it will be observed that when an adjective follows a noun in an oblique case, the case-ending is attached to the adjective.

Adjectives undergo no change of termination in order to agree in gender or number with the noun they qualify; *e.g.*—

"Găhàm hoásá," a good man.
"Găhàm hingzháusá," a good woman.

5.—Comparison.

The comparative degree of adjectives is denoted by (1) affixing the word "sári" (or "khri"), equivalent to our "than," to the word with which comparison is made; and (2) by appending the syllable "sin" to the adjective; as,—

"Bí áng-nŭ-khri găzaú sin," he is taller than I.

"Bê nŭá boi bangfáng-nŭ-sári găzaú sin," this house is higher than that tree.

It will be observed that—

(*a*)—The word "sári" or "khri" (=than) always takes the dative case before it; *e.g.*, "Boi" (or "boi-bŭ"), all; "Boi-nŭ-sári," than all.

(*b*)—The syllable of comparison "sin," attached to the adjective, is sometimes omitted.

(*c*)—The first syllable of the adjective is also occasionally omitted when comparison is made, *e.g.*—

"Áng-nŭ khri zaú-sin" (for "gŭzaú sin"), taller than I ("gŭzaú," tall).

The Superlative degree is expressed much in the same way, the noun (always in the dative case) being preceded by some word signifying *all:* "Boinŭ-sári bí gŭzaú′ sin," he is taller than all, or the tallest of all. The same sense may be conveyed in a slightly different way, as, "Boi-ni gęzráu bí gazaú siná," in the midst of (among) all he is the tallest; he is the tallest of all.

6.—Numeral Adjectives.

The numerals up to ten are as follows:—

One—Sè (sŭí).	Six—Ṛå (ḍå).
Two—Nè (nŭí).	Seven—Sni (sĭní).
Three—Thàm.	Eight—Skhô.
Four—Brè (brŭí).	Nine—Zàt.
Five—Bá.	Ten—Zŭ (zi).

No single words to express numbers above ten seem to be in common use; but the people sometimes avail themselves of the Assamese word for "score"—*kuri*, which in the mouth of a Kachári becomes "khuri." There is also a useful word to express a group of four, *i.e.*, "Za-khai" (= the Assamese গণ্ডা). This word when followed by two numerals is to be *multiplied* by the former, whilst the number represented by the latter is to be *added* to the result so obtained. In this way the Kacháris can express in their own language numbers up to 40 or 43, *e.g.*—

"Zakhai′ thàm (sá) thàm" = 4 × 3 + 3 = 15 (men).
"Zakhai′ zŭ (sá) nè" = 4 × 10 + 2 = 42 (men).

In the above examples it will be observed that the latter numeral is preceded by the word, "sá." This indicates a peculiarity in the use of numerals in Kachári. When several objects are spoken of, the noun designating them is usually placed first, and the word denoting their number follows, this latter being preceded by a word, usually monosyllabic, which serves to qualify, or rather classify, the objects referred to. There are a number of such prefixes in common use, among the best known being the following. To designate—

(*a*)—Human beings, "sá" is used (as above).
Three men, "Mànsŭí sá-thàm." Two boys, "Gâthâ sá-nè."

(*b*)—Irrational animals, "má."
Four goats, "Burmá má-brè." Five fowls, "Dáu mábá."

(*c*)—Fruits, rupees, and many *round* things, "thai."
"Thàkhá thai-bá," five rupees. "Thaizhu thai-brè," four mangoes.

(*d*)—Leaves (of trees or books), clothes, and various *flat* things, "gàng."
Three leaves, "Bilai gàng-thàm."

(*e*)—In some instances in words of two syllables, the latter part of the noun, or a word resembling it, is *repeated* before the numeral; *e.g.*—

"Bang-fàng fàng-thàm," three trees.
"Bidŭí dŭí-zŭ," ten eggs.

The above are some of the most frequently used of these particles, though there are others the usage of which cannot apparently be brought under any rule at present known. These can be learnt only by frequent practice in hearing and speaking.

III.—PRONOUNS.

Pronouns of five classes are found in Kachári,—*i.e.*, Personal, Relative, Interrogative, Demonstrative, and Adjective.

7.—Personal Pronouns.

These are as follows—

Singular.		*Plural.*	
1—Áng	... I.	Zang, or Zangfur (far)	we.
2—Nang	... thou.	Nang-sur (nang-sar)...	you.
3—Bí	... he, she, it.	Bí-sur (sar) (Bífar)...	they

These are declined in the same way as nouns; as—

Nom.—Áng (ángá)	... I.	Zang (zang-fur ; frá ; far)	we.
Obj.—Áng-khô	... me.	Zang-fur-khô	... us.
Instr.—Áng-zang	... by me.	Zang-fur-zang	... by us.
Dat.—Áng-nŭ	... to me.	Zang-fur-nŭ	... to us.
Abl.—Áng-ni-frai	... from me.	Zang-fur-ni-frai	... from us.
Poss.—Áng-ni, Áng-há	... of me.	Zang-fur-ni, Zang-fur-há	... of us.
Loc.—Áng-ni-áu	... in me.	Zang-fur-ni-áu	... in us.
Voc.—Helŭi áng	... O me!		

In the oblique cases of the plural number the syllable ("fur" or "frá") denoting number is sometimes omitted, and the case-sign affixed directly to the radical; *e.g.*, "Zang-ni," of us, instead of the full form, "Zang-fur-ni."

The declension of the pronouns of the second and third persons is perfectly regular. In their plural form, it will be observed that they often take the syllable "sur," instead of "fur," or "frá."

The pronoun of the third person knows no distinction of gender, he, she, it, being alike expressed by "bí."

Possession is denoted simply by using the personal pronoun in the possessive case, as—

"Bê *áng-ni* burmá," this is *my* goat.

8.—Relative Pronouns.

There seem to be no relative pronouns peculiar to the Kachári language, though "zi" and "zai," probably borrowed from their Hindú neighbours, are sometimes used; *e.g.*—

"Zi mànsŭí-khô áng miá nú-dang-man, bí khàṭ-láng-bai;"
The man I saw yesterday has run away.

This would be more idiomatically expressed by the use of the participle and omission of the relative pronoun; as—

"Miá (núnai) mànsŭí-á khàṭlàngbai;"
The man (seen) yesterday has run away.

9.—Interrogative Pronouns.

These are—

		Plural.
1.—Sur (sar)..	who ?	
2.—Má ...	what ?	Má-fur.
3.—Båbe ...	which ? (of several).	

These are declined like personal pronouns, but the first does not usually take the syllable ("fur") indicative of the plural number, when used to denote more than one.

10.—Demonstrative Pronouns.

These are—

Bê	... this.	Bê-sur (bê-fur)	... these.
Boi / Boi-há	} that.	Boi-sur (boi-fur)	... those.
Bí	... that (of *remote* distance).		

These may be declined in the usual way. Of the two forms of the plural given above, "sur" is used chiefly of human beings, and "fur" of all other objects—irrational animals, things, &c.

11.—Adjective Pronouns.

Some of the most common of these are—

Málai (of men) ...	other.	As many	... Zêsênŭ.
Gubun (of things)..		So many	... Têsênŭ.
Zábrá	... many.	How many (men)?	Sápsè (sábsè)?
Gaigai (gágai)	... each, self.	How many (animals)	Mápsè.
Surbá	... some one.	How many (rupees)	Thaipsè, *e.g.*—
Surbá surbá	... some (plural).		

How many rupees a month do you get?
"Dànfrimbo dànfrimbo thàkhá thaipsè manŭ?"

In the case of the last three words it will be observed that the interrogative pronoun, "how many," is expressed by the word "psè," the particles preceding it ("sá," "má," "thai," &c.) belonging to the order of classifying words always used in conjunction with numerals.—(*Vide* section on Numerals above).

IV.—VERBS.

12.—The verb is the most difficult part of the Kachári language to deal with, not so much from its structure or conjugation, which is perfectly regular, as from the fact that the usage and exact force of the different tenses is uncertain, some of these, especially those expressive of *past* time, being apparently sometimes used interchangeably. Again, the verb in Kachári admits of being compounded, not only with other verbal roots, but with adjectives, adverbs, and various affixes, which serve very materially to modify its meaning.

Every verb is conjugated from a verbal root or stem, which appears in its simplest form in the Imperative Mood, and which remains unchanged throughout all the different moods and tenses. This root or stem is in fact a verbal noun, and in composition sometimes takes the place of a noun, with the various case-endings, &c. The different relations of Tense, Mood, &c., are expressed by affixes attached directly to the verbal stem, an additional letter being occasionally inserted between the stem and the affix expressive of time, to prevent a disagreeable hiatus. Thus, the root "zá" (eat) when combined with "ŭ," the affix expressive of present (indefinite) time, becomes "záïŭ," he eats, the letter "ï" being no doubt inserted for the sake of euphony.

In Kachári the temporal affix retains its form unchanged in all three persons of both numbers. Thus the affix "bai," denoting past time, appended to the root, "tháng" (go), "tháng-bai," may be translated, "I (you, he, they) went." In such instances the number and person of the verb can only be determined by reference to the Nominative case, without regard to the exact form of the word.

13.—The following paradigm will give some insight into the method of conjugating the verb in Kachári, with the various affixes expressive of mood, tense, &c.

Conjugation of the regular verb active, "Nu-nŭ," to see.

Indicative Mood.

Simple Present—(Indefinite).

Singular.	*Plural.*				
1.—Áng	Zangfur	nuïŭ	I	we	see, seest, sees, &c.
2.—Nang	Nangsur		thou	you	
3.—Bí	Bísur		he	they	

Present Definite—(Progressive).

Nu-dang ... I, &c., am (art, is, are) seeing.

Simple Past.

Nu-bai ... I, &c., saw.

Past Progressive—(Imperfect).

Nu-dangman ... I, &c., was (wert, were) seeing, or, did see.

Past Remote—(Pluperfect).

Nu-nai
Nu-dangman } I, &c., had seen.

Simple Future.

Nu-gan ... I, &c., shall, or will see.

Paulo-post Future.

Nu-si-gan } I, &c., shall or will see (*i.e.*, almost imme-
Nu-nŭ-sŭí } diately).

IMPERATIVE MOOD.

Nu ... See thou (you).
Nu-thang ... Let him (them) see.

SUBJUNCTIVE MOOD.

Past or Future.

Nu-bá }If I see, or had seen.
Nu-blá }

POTENTIAL MOOD.

Simple Present.

Nu-nŭ hágaú ... I can see.

Simple Past.

Nu-nŭ hábai ... I could, &c., see.

Compound (Perfect) Past.

Nu-nŭ hágaúman ... I (may) might have seen.

Simple Future.

Nu-nŭ hágan ... I shall be able to see, &c., &c.

INFINITIVE MOOD.

Nu-nŭ ... To see.

PARTICIPLES.

Present.

Nu-ni ... Seeing.

Perfect.—(Conjunctive.)

Nu-ná-noi... Having seen.

Past.—(Generally with passive sense, but sometimes active.—*Cf. A.* "dekhá.")

Nu-nai ... Seen ; a seer.

AGENT.

Nu-grá ... One who sees, a seer [*H.*—Dekhne-wálá.]

14.—REMARKS ON THE MOODS, TENSES, &c.

A.—Little need be said regarding the Indicative, Infinitive, or Imperative Moods, as these are used much as in English. The Imperative Mood, it will be seen, admits of a lengthened form in the third person, "Nu-thang," let him (them) see.

The Subjunctive Mood has but two affixes ("bá," or "blá") which seem to be used indiscriminately to express past, present, or future time; as, "Áng bíkhô nubá angan," if I see him, I shall love (him). "Áng bíkhô nubá (nublá) angaúman," if I had seen him I should have loved (him).

The Potential Mood is expressed by means of the auxiliary verb, "Hánŭ," to be able. By subjoining the different temporal affixes to this root, "há," all the various degrees of past, present, and future time given for the Indicative Mood in the foregoing paradigm may be expressed.

Present time.—Two affixes are used to express present time, "ŭ" and "dang." Of these, the former is used somewhat indefinitely, in general statements, &c. "Bârâfrá zaú langŭ," the Kacháris drink *madh*. "Boi mansŭiá zaú langdang," that man is (now) drinking *madh*; the latter form indicating what is *definitely* going on at some point of present time. [*A.**—"Madh kháon": "Madh khaison."]

---

* In order to assist the learner, who may be assumed to know something of the Vernacular (Assamese) of the Upper Brahmaputra Valley, the Assamese equivalent of certain phrases, expressions, &c., is sometimes given in brackets, preceded by the letter *A*.

A third form of the present tense, only rarely met with, ends in "gô" (gaú.) This seems to be used frequently in answering questions affirmatively; *e.g.*, "Nang mithídang ná? Áng mithígô." Do you understand? (Yes), I understand.

Past time.—To express this, three affixes are used, "bai," "nai," and "dangman." Of these the first seems simply to express past time indefinitely; "Mikhàm zábai," I eat rice (*bhát*). The force of the affix, "dangman," is not quite clear, or definitely ascertained; it seems, indeed, to be used sometimes as an imperfect, sometimes as a pluperfect; as, "Bí fainaiáu, áng mikhàm zádangman," when he came I was eating (my) rice, (or, had eaten my rice?): this affix may, perhaps, be considered generally to express *remote past time.* The syllable, "nai," most commonly indicates the past participle ("Zánai," eaten), but is sometimes used in composition with the same force as "dangman," especially in interrogative sentences.

Future time.—This is expressed by the syllable "gan," affixed to the verbal root; as, "Bí faigan," he will come. The insertion of the syllable, "si," between the root and the affix serves to indicate a near future, or one about to become realised; "Bí fai-si-gan," he will come, *i.e.*, almost at once. [*A.*—"Áhibo lágise," he is about to come.] Much the same meaning seems to be given by the comparatively rare form, "nŭsŭí," or "nŭsè;" *e.g.*, "Áng fai-nŭ-sŭí," I am on the point of coming. This last form of the future tense is frequently used in asking questions, and may perhaps be looked upon as a kind of "interrogative future."

B.—Exceptional and irregular (abnormal) forms, &c.—

The Infinitive Mood is sometimes used with the force of the Indicative, especially in asking questions; *e.g.*—

"Khamsiáu mábrŭí thángnŭ," how can I go in the dark? "Mánŭ gínŭ," why should I be afraid?

These expressions are perhaps elliptical, the Infinitive verb being governed by some other verb understood; *e.g.*, the latter sentence might be fully expressed thus:—

"Mánŭ gínŭ, (nánggô)," why (is it necessary for me) to fear?

An exceptional form of the present tense is that ending in "ni;" this form is of comparatively rare occurrence, and is used only in the *first* person; *e.g.*—

"Áng { thang-ŭ" / tháng-ni" } I go.

Past time is occasionally expressed by the affix "khŭ" (khu), the use of this form of the verb being confined chiefly to *interrogative* sentences; *e.g.*—

"Hingzháusá mobá { faibai" / faikhŭ" } When did the woman come?

C.—Use of the Participles, &c.—

The participle is frequently used as a verbal noun, and as such may take the usual case-endings, &c., in composition; *e.g.*—

"Bíni lítnai-á hàmá," his writing is bad.

"Nangni hábá máunaikhô áng hàmá manŭ," I do not like your work (*lit.*, I find your work bad. [*A.*—Tômár kám bêá páôn]. ("Lítnai-á," past participle of "lítnŭ," to write, with sign of nominative case "á" appended. "Máunai-khô," past participle of "máunŭ," to do, with sign of objective case "attached).

This past participle in "nai" is used very largely, and may bear either an active or passive sense; *e.g.*—

"Áng miá nunai gâthâá thángbai," the boy whom I saw (*lit.*, seen [by] me) yesterday went away. [*A.*—Moi káli dekhá lârá gol].

"Ángkhô miá nunai gâthâá thángbai," the boy who saw me yesterday went away. [*A.*—Môk káli dekhá lârá gol].

This participle is often used also to denote the agent or doer of the action expressed by the verb, as in the latter of the two preceding illustrations; *e.g.*—

"Mai hánaifur dá mikhàm zádang," the reapers (*lit.*, the paddy-cutters) are now eating their dinner.

The same meaning (agent) may be expressed in another way by appending the affix "grá" to the verbal root; *e.g.*—

"Manaiáu mai hágráfur miánggan," in the evening the reapers will be tired.

This participle is sometimes combined with a noun to form a compound adjective qualifying another noun; *e.g.*—

"Bê hábá máu-sŭ-nai mànsŭí," this (is) a very hard-working (*lit.*, much-work-doing) man. ("Sŭ," intensive particle = very).

A kind of participial adverb is sometimes used, formed by attaching the affix "ŭí" to the verbal root; thus, the root, "miní" (laugh, smile) + ŭí, = smilingly; *e.g.*, "Miníŭí miníŭí khoráng khithábai," he spoke smilingly, *i.e.*, he continued to smile all the time he was speaking. (This seems to be the full force of the reduplicated participial adverb).

15.—Passive Voice.

A.—The Passive voice is formed simply by prefixing the past participle of the Regular verb to the different tenses of the Substantive verb, "Záanŭ," to be, become. A synopsis of the conjugation of this verb, which is quite regular, is here given.

	PRESENT.		PAST.		IMPERFECT.	FUTURE.
	Simple.	*Definite.*	*Simple.*	*Remote.*		
Ind.	Záaïŭ.	Záadang.	Záabai.	Záanai (záadangman).	Záadangman.	Záagan.
Imp.	Záa. Záathang.					
Subj.	Záabá. (Záablá).					
Pot.	Záanŭ-hágaú.	Záanŭ-hádang.	Záanŭ-hábai.	Záanŭ-hábai (hádangman).	Záanŭ-hádangman.	Záanŭ-hágan.
Infin.	Záanŭ.					
Part.	Záani.	......	Záanánoi.	Záanai.		

In order to give the conjugation of the Passive voice of any verb, we have simply to prefix the past participle of that verb to the different tenses of the verb "Záanŭ" above given. Thus, "Nunŭ," to see: past participle, "nunai," seen; "Áng nunai záaïŭ," I am seen; "Áng nunai záabai," I was seen; "Áng nunai záagan," I shall be seen, &c.

B.—Cognate in meaning to the verb "Záanŭ" is the defective verb "Dang" (danga), am, art, is, are. Only two tenses of this verb are in use, the present, "Dang," is; and imperfect, "Dangman," was; and by the help of these, certain tenses (present definite and past remote) of the regular verb are formed. They are also used independently in narrative [*H.*—Hai, thá]; "Gámiáu bårá sásè dangman," there was an old man in the village. Sometimes the verbal root is omitted, and only the temporal affix retained; as, "Áng khansè gåthå man" (man = dangman), I was once a boy.

16.—NEGATIVE VERBS.

A.—The conjugation of the Negative verb is peculiar, and differs materially from that of the Regular verb. A negative force is given to the verb, not in the way common to many languages, *i.e.*, by *prefixing* a negative adverb ("na," "ne," "non," &c.=not), but by *attaching* an affix directly to the verbal stem. Some of the forms assumed by the verb when conjugated in a negative sense, will appear from the following synopsis of the verb, "Nunŭ," to see, in its negative form :—

	PRESENT.	PAST. Simple.	PAST. Remote.	IMPERFECT. PLUPERFECT.	FUTURE.
Ind.	Nuá.	Nuákhŭínŭ nuáman.	Nuákhŭísè.	Nuákhŭíman.	Nuá.
Imp.	Dá nu. Dá nuthang.				
Subj.	Nuábá.	(Nuáblá).			
Pot.	Nunŭ haiá.	Nunŭ haiákhŭísè. Nunŭ haiákhŭínŭ.		....	Nunŭ haiá.
Part.	Nuï.	Nuë.	(Nuálábá.)		

B.—It will be observed that a negative force is given to the root "Nu" (see) by attaching to it the affix "á" throughout the different moods and tenses. In certain cases this termination "á" becomes "ï" or "ë," especially in participial constructions ; *e.g.*, "Bíkhô nu-ï-khai, áng faifáfinbai," I came back because I did not see him. "Bíkhô nuálábá áng faifáfinbai," I came back without having seen him.

This latter form of the negative verb (combined with "lábá") is a kind of participial adverb, and is of frequent use in Kachári, as is the analogous expression in Assamese ; *e.g.*, "Nualábá"=*A.*—Ná dekhákoi ; "Gabáu khàmálábá"=*A.*—Palam na karákoi ; "Aná lábá"=*A.*—Maram na karákoi, &c., &c.

17.—CAUSATIVE VERBS.

A.—These are formed generally by appending the verb "Hŭnŭ," to give, to the infinitive mood of the principal verb, the various relations of mood and tense being indicated by the usual temporal affixes attached to this root "Hŭ," give: the conjugation of this causative form of the verb is quite regular.

Synopsis of the verb, "Nunŭ hŭnŭ" [*A.*—Dekhibo díá, dekhúá], to cause to see, to show:—

	Present. Simple.	Present. Definite.	Past. Simple.	Past. Remote.	Future.
Ind.	Nunŭ hŭĭŭ.	Nunŭ hŭdang.	Nunŭ hŭbai.	Nunŭ hŭdangman.	Nunŭ hŭgan.
Imp.	Nunŭ hŭ. ——— hŭthang.				
Subj.	Nunŭ hŭbá. / hŭblá.	Nunŭ hŭdangbá.	Nunŭ hŭbaibá.	Nunŭ hŭdangmanbá.	Nunŭ hŭbá; nuhŭbá.
Pot.	Nuhŭnŭ hágaú.	...	Nu hŭnŭ hábai.	Nu hŭnŭ hádangman.	Nu hŭnŭ hágan.
Part.	Nunŭ hŭbá.	...	Nunŭ hŭnánoi.		

B.—In some instances a simple verb acquires a causative force by undergoing a slight change of FORM, in the way of *addition* or otherwise, usually in its *first* syllable; *e.g.*—

Salangnŭ, to learn.	Farangnŭ, to cause to learn, to teach.
Ránnŭ, to dry (neuter).	Frànnŭ, to cause to dry, to dry (active).
Dugúĭnŭ, to bathe (oneself).	Thukúĭnŭ, to bathe (others).
Sínŭ, to become wet (cloth, &c.)	Fsínŭ, to cause to be wet, soak, steep, &c.

C.—*Relation of Cause and Effect.*—This is expressed by means of the word "khai" [*A.*—Káran], which usually takes the possessive case before it, except when it is preceded by a verb or participle, when the sign of the possessive case is commonly omitted; *e.g.*—

"Bíni khai faibai," on that account, I came.

"Sándung gabráb khai áng thángnŭ haiákhŭísè," because the sun was strong, I could not go.

18.—Compound Verbs.

These are very numerous, verbal roots being compounded with Adjectives, Adverbs, other verbal roots, and various particles expressive of number, completeness, &c., which often materially qualify the meaning of the original verbal root. Thus the verb "Záanŭ," to be, is often compounded with the qualifying word, "găhàm," which is either adjective or adverb (good, or well), the first syllable of the qualifying word being generally omitted, and the various modal and temporal affixes being then attached directly to the shortened form "hàm."

Conjugation of the compound verb, "Hàmnŭ" (for "găhàm záanŭ") [*A.*—Bhál hôá], to be good, to be well:—

	Present.		Past.		Future.
	Simple.	*Definite.*	*Simple.*	*Remote.*	
Ind.	Hàmŭ.	Hàmdang.	Hàmbai.	Hàmdang-man.	Hàmgan.
Imp.	Găhàm záa. ——— záathang.				
Subj.	Hàm bá.	Hàmdang-bá.	Hàmbai-bá.	Hàmdang-manbá.	Hàmgan-bá.
Pot.	Hàmnŭ	— hágaú.	Hàmnŭ hábai.	Hàmnŭ hádangman.	Hàmnŭ hágan.
Part.	Hàmbá.	Hàmni.	Găhàm záanai găhàmnai.		

It will be observed that, with the exception of the Imperative Mood, both members of the compound verb are used in an abbreviated form throughout, the root of the verb ("Záa") for the most part disappearing altogether, and the temporal affixes being attached directly to the last syllable of the adjective. Thus, "Hàmgan" [*A.*—Bhál hobo] would in its full form be, "Găhàm záagan," it will (be) well. This rule apparently holds good in most, if not all, cases where adjectives are compounded with verbs; as, "Thaúgan," it will (be) deep, (for "Găthaú záagan"); "Horá thaúdang," (for "Găthaú záadang,") the night is deepening.

19.—Verbs are frequently compounded with other verbs, the two *roots* only in such cases being combined, and the modal and temporal affixes being attached directly to the latter root; thus the verb, "Fàfinnŭ," to turn, is very frequently attached to such roots, as, "Thàng," go; "Fai," come; "Lábo," bring; "Hŭ," give, &c.; and this combination gives us such useful words, as—

Áng	tháng fai lábo hŭ, &c.	fáfingan, I will	go come bring give, &c.	back.

In such compounds (verbal) the *second* root often indicates the *result* of the compound action indicated by the whole verb, while the *former* root shows the *manner* in which this result is brought about. Thus, the root "Thàṭ" (to kill), when preceded by another root, indicates not only "death by violence," but the *mode* of death; *e.g.*—

Bú (beat) Su (pierce) Saú (bruise) Dàn (cut) Gáu (shoot), &c., &c.	thàṭnŭ	to beat —pierce —bruise — cut —shoot, &c.,	to death.

There are several other particles in the language attached to verbal roots to form compound verbs after the analogy of the above examples. Some of those most commonly used, with their significations, are given here—

(*a*)—"Láng" denotes completeness, or intensifies the sense of the simple verb; *e.g.*—

Goraiá	khàtdang khàt-láng-dang	the horse is	running. running away.

(*b*)—"Bai" expressed *continuous*, progressive action:—

Dáuá	bíṛdang bíṛ-bai-dang	the bird is	flying. flying about continually.

(*c*)—"Zlai" is used of *reflexive, reciprocal* action :—

"Sŭímá âṭgan," the dog will bite.

"Sŭímáfrá âṭ-zlai-gan," the dogs will bite each other.

20A.—Verbs are occasionally combined even with nouns, though such combinations are comparatively rare. The verbal root "Záa" (be, become), is the one most commonly used in such compounds, the root itself often being elided, and the temporal affix being attached directly to the noun. The following illustrations will give some idea of the general principle on which such compounds are formed :—

"Maná," evening; "Manágan (=maná záagan)," it will (be) evening: *lit.*, "It will eve."

"Khamsi," darkness; "Khamsibái (=khamsi záabai)," it has (darkened) become dark.

"Khamsinŭ nàmaidang (=khamsi záanŭ nàmaidang" [*A.*—Endhár hobo khúzise], it is about to (become) dark.

In such instances it will be seen that the verbal root "Záa" (be) disappears altogether, the temporal affix only remaining, and combining with the substantive to form a kind of verbal noun. These verbal nouns may be conjugated throughout by attaching the modal and temporal affixes given in the foregoing paradigms.

20B.—Verbs are sometimes combined with other parts of speech; *e.g.*, Adverbs, as—

"Bebai'diblá áng thánggan," under the circumstances, I shall go. (*Lit.*—If it is so, I shall go.)

"Bebaidi núngábá, áng thángá," under other circumstances I shall not go. (*Lit.*—If it is not so, I shall not go).

In these sentences "Bebaidi" is the Adverb, "thus," [*A.*—Ene], with which "blá" (shortened form of "záablá," from "záanŭ," to be, is combined [*A.*—Ene hole]; while "nungabá," is the Subjunctive Mood of the emphatic negative verb "núngá." (22). [*A.*—Ene na hole].

21.—Completive (intensive) Verbs.

A.—A common usage in Kachári is to strengthen and intensify the meaning of a verbal root by attaching a distinct syllable to it, this syllable being inserted *between* the verbal stem and the temporal affix throughout the conjugation. The particles most commonly employed for this purpose are, "khàng," "zap" ("zab"), "tra," "sŭ," &c. The following illustrations will give some indication of the general principle on which such compounds are used :—

"Mai hábai," (he) has cut his paddy.
"Mai há-*khàng*-bai," (he) has *finished* cutting his paddy [*A.*—Dhán dai êtálê].

"Boi gámini mànsŭífrá thoibai," the men of that village died.
"Boi gámini mànsŭífrá boibŭ thoi-*tra*-bai," the men of that village *all* died out: *i.e.*, to a man.

In such instances as the last given, not only is the "particle of completeness" attached to the verbal stem, but some adjective of the same purport is often used with the noun ("tra; boibŭ"=all.)

The particle (intensive) "su" is often used in the same way, as—

"Bàr bàr-dang," the wind is blowing.
"Bàr bàr-*sŭ*-dang," the wind is blowing *strongly*.

In other combinations the same particle is used to express large *numbers* (=adverb, "many," &c.); *e.g.*—

"Bê nŭáu thàmfoi dang-a," there are mosquitoes in this house.
"———————dang-*sŭ*-ī-a," there are *many* mosquitoes in this house.

{ "Lámaiáu mànsŭifur fai-dang," men are coming along the road.
"———————— fai-*sŭ*-dang," *many* men, &c., &c.

B.—In some few instances the noun is repeated in the verb when this latter stands in a specially close—almost technical—relation to the noun; *e.g.*—

"Bê bangfángá (fi*thai thai*gan,") this tree (will bear fruit.) *Lit.*, will fruit fruit.

"Dáuá (bi*dŭi dŭi*dang,") the hen (is laying eggs).

"Sànfrimbo (*bàr bàrŭ*,") (the wind blows) every day. (*Cf.*—"The *rain it raineth* every day.")

22.—Defective Verbs, Auxiliary Verbs, &c.

A.—These are not numerous in Kachári. The most common is that already noticed, *viz.*:—

"Danga, dangman," is, was,—used apparently only in the present and imperfect tenses; and its negative "Gŭiá," is not, was not.

"Bê gámiáu mànsŭi danga ná? Gŭiá," are there men in this village? There are not.

A strongly *emphatic* form of the negative "gŭiá" is formed by inserting the particle "li" after the first syllable; *e.g.*—

"Bê gámiáu mànsŭi gŭi-*li*-á," there is not *even* a *single* man in this village.

This word "gŭiá," like its correlative "gnáng" (see below) is sometimes appended to nouns to form a compound adjective; *e.g.*—

"Bê thàkhá gŭiá," he is without money,—poor.

"Bê thàkhá gnáng," he is possessed of money,—rich.

When used in this way the termination of the word sometimes undergoes a slight change, and it may take the form "gŭiё" or "gŭii," &c.

Another form of the negative verb substantive is "núngá," which is perhaps somewhat more emphatic than "gŭiá."

"Bê gámiáu *hoásá* danga ná ? Núngá ; *hingzháusá* danga."
Are there *men* in this village ? No, (but) there are *women.*

As a general rule { Gŭiá / Núngá } is equivalent to the Assamese { Nai. / Na hoi.

B.—Necessity, obligation, &c.—

Physical necessity is expressed by the word, "náng-gô" (nanggaú) ;—in its negative form, "náng-á" [*A.*—Láge ;—ná láge] ; as,—

"Nang bê hábá máuanŭ nánggô," you must do this work.
"Nang sànáu udúnŭ nángá," you must not sleep in the daytime.

Moral necessity (duty, right and wrong, &c.) is expressed either by (*a*) the adjectives, "gahàm," "hàmá," good, bad ; or (*b*) the verb, "mannŭ" [*A.*—Pábo], which in its negative form become "man-á"; as—

"Zangfur bizang bêzang hahai hŭnaiá gahàm," we ought to help each other.

"Mànsŭiá sikháu { khàmnŭ maná" / khámnaiá hàmá" } men must not steal.

Connected etymologically perhaps with the verb "Nánggó," is the useful particle "gnáng" [*A.*—Lagiá], which denotes (1) possession, &c., as, "Thàkhá gnáng," possessed of rupees, *i.e.*, wealthy ; and (2) necessity, moral obligation, &c. ; *e.g.*—

"Máunŭ gnáng hábá" [*A.*—Koribo lagia karam], duty—"what (we) ought to do."
"Mannŭ gnáng" [*A.*—Pábo lagia], rights—"what (we) ought to get."

Most of these verbs, though here called defective, admit of being conjugated to a certain extent with the usual modal and temporal affixes ; *e.g.*—

"Ban gŭíábá mikhàm sŭngnŭ haiá;"

If there is no firewood, (I) cannot cook (my) rice.

"Gŭíábá" is here the subjunctive mood of "gŭíá."

23.—ADVERBS.

In the Kachári language are found adverbs of Manner, Time, and Place.

A.—Adverbs of Manner *(quality)*.

These in many cases are formed from the cognate adjective simply by adding "hŭí," or "ŭí;" as "găhàm," good; "gahàmhŭí," well; "hàmá," bad; "hàmèhŭí," badly. When the adjective ends in a vowel (as in the latter illustration), the termination often undergoes a slight change before the adverbial affix is attached.

Some of the Adverbs of Manner in most common use are the following:—

Mámàr / Gakhrŭí .... quickly.
Mábrŭí .... how? in what way?
Bebaidi .... in this way.
Boibaidi .... in that way.
Zeroi hágaŭ .... somehow.
Zábrá .... many.
Bángai .... few.
Làsè làsè [*A.*—Làhe làhe].. slowly, gradually.
Mohábá .... somewhere.
Balŭ; búá .... only.
Bábŭ (affix) theobŭ .... although.
Bifar màni .... et cetera (&c.) [*A.*—Ádi kari.]
Gamáinŭ .... certainly, surely.
Thápnŭ .... suddenly.
Mábábrŭíbá .... in some way or other.
Hàtsingŭí .... alone.

B.—Adverbs of Time.

Díni	to-day.
Gábun	to-morrow.
Míá	yesterday.
Dákháli	day before yesterday
Sŭpnchá	day after to-morrow.
Dá	now.
Dásŭ, dánŭ (emphatic)	even now, at once.
Mobá	when ?
Zeblá, ablá	when, then.
Azai ; azainŭ	always.
Unáu	afterwards.
Fúngáu ; fúngzáni	in the morning.
Áglá	before.
Zebláhálági—abláhálági	as long as—so long.
Khansè	once.
Khanlè khanlè	often, frequently.
Teblá	then (of time.
Abá ; bibáidiblá	then (of argument.
Hálági ; zebláhálági	until.
Amphá ; amphàre	then ; afterwards.

Many of these adverbs of time can be made emphatic by the addition of certain enclitic syllables ; *e.g.*—

" Dá," now ; " dásŭ," even now, at this very moment.

Some of them also admit of being declined as nouns, as, " Dánifrai áng nangkhô angan," from this time I shall love you. Here, " dá " (= now) has the force of a noun (this time), in the ablative case.

C.—Adverbs of Place.

Beáunŭ .... here ; *i.e.*, in this (place)
Boiáunŭ .... there ; *i.e.*, in that (place).
Mohá (maúhá) .... where ?
Gezráu .... within.
Báizzháu .... without.
Sĭgáng (sŭgáng).............. before.
Unáu .... behind.
Khàthiáu .... near.
Sááu (saiáu) .... above.
Singáu .... below.
Găzàn .... afar.

Many of these, it will be seen, are simply nouns in the Locative case, and as such they admit of being declined ; as,—

"Bí Tezpur khàthinifrai faidang," he comes from near Tezpur.

Here, "khàthi" (=near) has the force of a noun (="neighbourhood," &c.,) in the ablative case.

24.—PREPOSITIONS (POSTPOSITIONS).

The words corresponding to what we call "prepositions" are in Kachári for the most part placed *after* the noun, and might, therefore, be more properly called "postpositions." Some of these have been already referred to as forming the case-endings in the declension of nouns. Others in common use are the following :—

Lagŭsò .... together with.
Khai........................ on account of ; [*A.*—Káraṅ.]
Gezráu .... in the midst.
Há lági .... up to, as far as.
Baidi .... like.
Fàtbrŭíthing .... All around ; [*A.*—Chário fále).

Most of these require the possessive case before them, as—

"Boi-ni khai áng thángnŭ haiá-khŭísè,"
On account of that I could not go.

The sign of the possessive case is sometimes omitted, as—

"Gazángnai khai áng thángnŭ haiá,"
On account of the cold I cannot go.

"Gazángnai" is here the past tense of neuter verb, "Gazángnŭ," to be cold, used as a verbal noun,—a construction in which the sign of the possessive case is usually omitted.

25.—CONJUNCTIONS.

Conjunctions are used but sparingly in Kachári, their place in this, as in other Oriental languages, being largely taken by participles, &c. This is especially the case with some of the conjunctions of most frequent occurrence, such as "and," "if," &c.; *e.g.*—

"Áng bíkhô nunánoi lingbai," I saw him and called him. (*Lit.*, I seeing him, called him).

"Áng bíkhô nubá linggan," if I see him, I will call him. (*Lit.*, I on seeing him, will call him).

Other conjunctions sometimes met with are given below, some of these (to which [*A.*] is prefixed) are obviously adopted from the Assamese :—

[*A.*]—Árŭ, o (affix) bŭ .... and, also, too.
Mánathŭ ; khai .... because ; for, &c.
[*A.*]—Khintu ; theobŭ .... but, however, &c.
Núngábá ; zaiábá .... else, otherwise.
Anthaibá ; bá.................. or.
Bábŭ (affix) ; theobŭ ...... although.
Bíni khai .... therefore.
Bá ; blá (affixes) .... if.

26.—INTERJECTIONS.

These are but little used; some of the most common are—

Sri, sri .... hush! be silent!
Hâânoi; naisung.................. look! look!
[A.]—Hai, hai .... alas!
Núnggô .... yes, certainly (strong affirmative).
Găhàm............................ well done!
Helŭi .... hallo! oh!

27.—WORDS BORROWED FROM OTHER LANGUAGES.

In Kachári, as in many other uncultivated languages, many of the words dealing with subjects rising above the sphere of daily wants and wishes, are adopted from the speech of their more civilised neighbours. Accordingly, words obviously taken from the Assamese, Bengáli, Hindustáni, and even English languages, are not unfrequently used, especially in written composition. Such foreign words almost always undergo certain changes in the mouth of a Kachári, and among the most obvious of such changes are the following:—

A.—A nasal sound is often inserted where the original Áryan word has none; *e.g.*, "Kathál" (jack-tree) becomes "Kanthál."

B.—An unaspirated initial consonant is very commonly, though not invariably, aspirated; *e.g.*, "Taká" (rupee) becomes "thàkhá" (or "thànkhá," a nasal being sometimes inserted); "pur" (whole, complete), "fur;" "prabháu" (glory, might), "frabháu."

Occasionally the reverse process takes place, an initial aspirated consonant giving place to an unaspirated one; *e.g.*, "Ghorá" (horse) becomes "gorai."

In other cases, usually in words of more than two syllables, an aspirated consonant at the beginning of a word is transferred to a similar position in the second syllable of the word; *e.g.*, "Bhitarat" (within, inside) becomes "bitharáu," &c.

C.—The dental sounds "d," "t," &c., are usually replaced by others of a *cerebral* character, closely approximating to the sounds of the corresponding English letters.

D.—The various sibilant letters, "s," "sh," &c., are commonly replaced by "kh," which often becomes a strong *guttural* aspirate; *e.g.*, "Ásá" (hope), "ákhá," &c.

PART III.—SYNTAX.

With the limited knowledge of the Kachári language at present available, it would be idle, and probably misleading, to attempt to lay down a complete sketch of the syntax of this form of non-Áryan speech. Indeed, much of what is known of this part of the subject has been already anticipated in the Accidence. Perhaps the best method of obtaining some insight into the syntax of the language is the careful study and analysis of a certain number of typical and illustrative sentences, which may serve to show the changes and modifications undergone by the different parts of speech when brought into syntactical relation with each other. In the following pages a number of such sentences are given, arranged in groups, following the order of the different parts of speech, and numbered with reference to the sections bearing the same numbers in the Accidence. In this way it is hoped that some of the leading syntactical principles of the language will be brought before the student, his attention being specially drawn to these principles by enclosing the typical and representative word or phrase in parentheses, in English and Kachári alike. Occasionally, explanatory notes are added, and sometimes attempts are made to lay down formal rules, though these latter, with the limited knowledge of the language at present at the writer's command, cannot pretend to be more than *approximately* correct.

I.—NOUNS.

1.—Gender.

(The boys and girls) are coming. (Gâthâ gâthaifrá) faidang.

(The cock) is crowing ... (Dáu zlaiá) gŭsípdang.

(The hen) lay eggs ... (Dau zŭá) bidŭí dŭiŭ.

The (he-goat) eats grass ... (Burmá fànthaiá) gángsŭ záiŭ.

The (she-goat) gives milk ... (Burmá fànthiá) gákhir hŭiŭ.

The (boar) is very fierce ... (Omá bundaiá) khepzràng.

This (sow) has four young ones. Bê (omá bundihá) fĭsá mábrŭí danga.

2.—Number.

The (man) is dying ... (Mànsŭiá) thoidang.

All (men) will die ... Boibŭ (mánsŭifur) thoigan.

The (boy) laughs ... (Gâthâá) mĭnídang.

(Boys) like to play ... (Gâthâfur) gelenŭ gŭhàm manŭ.

The (tiger) lives in jungle ... Mosaiá hágraiáu tháiŭ.

(Tigers) eat goats ... (Mosáfrá) burmáfurkhô záiŭ.

The (dog) is barking ... (Sŭímaiá) sangdang.

The (dogs) are fighting together. (Sŭímáfrá) bízang bêzang nángzláidang.

3.—Case.

The (men) have come ... (Mànsŭífur) faibai.

The (boy) is sleeping ... (Gâthâá) udúdang.

The (dog) will bite ... (Sŭímaiá) atgan.

(Birds) fly ... (Dáufur) bírbaiiŭ.

Light the (fire) ... (Åt) sukháng.

Cook the (rice) ...	(Mikhàm) sang.
Honour your (father and mother).	(Nammá namfákhô) mányŭ klàm.
I will shoot (a tiger) ...	Áng (mosákhô) gáuthátgan.
Cut down the tree (with an axe).	(Ruázang) bangfàngkhô dàn.
I catch fish (with a net) ...	Áng (zê zang) ná hamŭ.
He shot the bird (with a gun)	Bí dáukhô (sĭlai zang) gáuthàṭbai.
Men cut paddy (with a sickle)	(Khási zang) mànsŭífur mai háiŭ.
Give (me) some rice ...	Mikhàm bángai (ángnŭ) hŭ.
I will give (you) ten rupees a month.	Dànfrimbo dànfrimbo* (nangnŭ) thàkhá thaizŭ hŭgan.
Bring (him) some firewood...	(Bínŭ) bángai ban lábo.
I gave (them) some water ...	Áng (bisúrnŭ) bángai dukhô hŭbai.
Take the knife (from him) ...	(Bínifrai) khàthrikhô sê'nánoi láng.
I am bringing rice (from the bazaar).	(Bazárnifrai) mairang lábodang.
I bought this cloth (from a shop-keeper).	(Dukhánnifrai) bê híkhô bainánoi lábobai.
He comes (from Tezpur) ...	Bí (Tezpurnifrai) faidang.
I can do (my) work ...	(Ángni) hábákhô khàmnŭ hágaú.
Is the fruit (of that tree) good?	(Boi bangfàngni) fithai găhàm ná?
The thatch (of the house) is rotten.	(Nŭni) thoriá sêaúbai.
(His) wife is ill ...	(Bíni) hingzháuá zobará zádang.

* This is a "reduplicative" and distributive form of speech, like "Rôz rôz" (day by day) in Hindustáni.

The (tiger's) claws are sharp	(Mosáni). àsúgur gabaú.
(I have) [of me] ten rupees	(Ánghá) thàkhá thaizŭ danga.
Stay (in the house) ...	(Nŭáu) thá.
Fish live (in the water) ...	Naiá (dŭïáu) tháïŭ.
Snakes are found (in the grass)	Zibaúfur (gáng'sŭïáu) man-nai záïŭ.
There are three cows (in the field).	Mosaúfur máthàm (dubliáu) danga.
(O my friend), come quickly	(Helŭi khurmá), mámàr fai.
(O sir), give me a little rice...	(Hai sáhib), ángnŭ bángai mikhàm hŭ.

Order of Words in a Sentence.—This generally follows the rule common in many other languages; *i.e.*, 1, Subject; 2, Object; 3, Verb. Of the qualifying and subordinate words, the adjective may either follow or precede its noun, whilst the adverb is used before its verb or adjective, and what we call prepositions almost invariably follow the nouns they govern. Occasionally the verb is placed first and the subject at the end of the sentence, this being done when very great emphasis is given to the action of the verb; *e.g.*, "Sŭímá aṯgan," the dog will bite (non-emphatic). "Aṯganthŭ (aṯgandè) sŭímaiánŭ," *bite* the dog (most certainly) will—(strongly emphatic.)

In this last (emphatic) form of the sentence it will be observed that both subject and verb take certain affixes, "thŭ" and "dè" in the case of the verb, and "ánŭ" in the case of the noun, the latter being, in fact, a compound affix (á + nŭ), the former part (á) having to some extent the force of the definite article, and the latter (nŭ) being an "enclitic" particle. Other affixes of this character are "bŭ" (bo) and "sŭ" (so) "sŭí" (soí), the latter being used chiefly with verbs, whilst "bŭ" and "nŭ" are attached to adjectives (adverbs) and nouns (pronouns), &c. These affixes, which may perhaps be called "euphonic enclitics," seem to be used for a double purpose,—partly for the sake of euphony and partly to strengthen and emphasise the meaning of the words to which they are attached. In some cases they seem to affect the meaning of a word or sentence very slightly if at all, and their use is then mainly euphonic: and it may be observed *generally* that *considerations of euphony have great weight in determining the exact form and structure of words and sentences in this language.*

4.—ADJECTIVES.

A (high) mountain ...	Házu (găzaú).
(Deep) water ...	Dŭí (găthaú).
The plantain is (sweet) ...	Thálidá { gătháu.* / gădoi.* }
The bamboo is (long) ...	Oá (gălau).
The elephant is (strong) ...	Háthiá (balágrá).

5.—Comparison.

The elephant is (stronger than the horse).	(Goráinŭ khri) háthiá (balágrá).
Your dog is (better than mine)	Ángni (sŭímánŭkhri) nangni sŭímá (găhàm).
Man is (taller than) woman...	(Hingzháunŭkhri) hoáiá (găzaú).
You are (worse than) I am...	Nang (ángnŭkhri hàmá).
The elephant is (the largest of all beasts).	(Boibo zanthu'nŭkhri) háthiá (gădet'siná).
He is the (best of the boys)...	(Boibo găthâ'nŭsá"ri) bí (găhàmsiná).
He is the (worst of all) ...	Bí (boinŭsári hàmá'siná).
The Brahmaputra is a (*very large*) river.	Brahmaputra dŭimáiá† (gădetsin).

* { "Găthấu," [A.—Huád], sweet to taste
"Gădoi," sweet in *broad*, *general* sense.

† { Dŭí-má = river (large)
Dŭí-sá = rivulet } { "sá" "diminutive" affix, opposed to "má." (*Cf.* Mai-má, "bar dhán;" Mai-sá, "horu dhán," &c.)

6.—Numeral Adjectives (Classifying Numerals).

(Five men) are working ...	(Sábá mànsŭíá) hábá máudang.
Bring (seven fishes) ...	(Másĭní ná) lábo.
I killed three dogs ...	·Sŭímá máthàm buthàṭbai.
Buy (ten eggs) for (five pice)	(Faisá gatbá) hŭnánoi (bidŭí dŭízŭ) bai.
I got (two goats) for (three rupees).	(Thaitham thàkhá) hŭnánoi áng (mánŭí burmá) manbai.
There are (fifteen trees) in this field.	Bê dubliáu (bangfàng zŭhkai' thàm fàngthàm) danga.
The cow has (two horns) ...	Mosaúhá (gang mannŭí) danga.

PRONOUNS.

7.—Personal Pronouns.

(I) can walk ...	(Áng) thábainŭ hágaú.
(He) struck (me) with a cane	Raigan zang (bí) (ángkhô) bubai.
Give (me) the rice [*sául*] ...	Mairangkhô (ángnŭ) hŭ.
Take (it from me) ...	(Ángnifrai bíkhô) láng.
(We) can see (you) ...	(Zangfur nangkhô) nainŭ hágaú.
(They) saw (us) ...	(Bísur zangfurkhô) nubai.
Go (to them) ...	(Bisur'niáu) tháng.
(I) came (from them) ...	(Áng) (bisur'nifrai) faibai.
Show (them to us) ...	(Bisurkhô zangfur'niáu) naihŭ.
Did (you) call (us)? ...	(Nang zangfurkhô) lingnai ná?
(My) son is coming ...	(Ángui) fĭsá faidang.
(His) house is large ...	(Bíni) nŭá gădít.

Reduplicative use of the Personal Pronoun.—When a personal pronoun is used in the possessive case, it is sometimes repeated in a slightly changed form before the noun it qualifies, especially when this latter expresses intimate family relationship, *e.g.*, father, mother, brother, &c., thus—

My	father	Ángni á-fá.	My	mother	Ángni ái.
Your		Nangni nang-fá.	Your		Nangni nam-má.
His		Bíni bí-fá.	His		Bíni bí-má.

Here the words "father" and "mother" are represented by the monosyllables, "fá" and "má;" but when preceded by a pronoun in the possessive case, that pronoun is *repeated* before these nouns,—in the first person its form undergoing a certain change, "áfá" being substituted for "áng-fá" (my father), and "ái" for "áng-má" (my mother). This rule holds good of other nouns of the same class; *e.g.*, "dá," eldest son of a family [*A.*—Kakái], takes the forms "á-dá," "nang-dá," "bí-dá"; "bå," eldest daughter, becomes, "á-bå," "nang-bå," "bí-bå," &c., &c.

8, Relative; 9, Interrogative; 10, Demonstrative; and 11, Adjective Pronouns.

8.—The man (who) came brought rice.	(Zainŭ) faibai, bí mairang lábobai.
Send him (whom) you may meet.	(Zaikhô) lagŭ mangan, bíkhô thinhat.
Return the rupee to (him who lost) it.	Thàkhá (gamánaikhô) hŭfin.
The boy (who) worked yesterday is dead.	(Zai) gåthåá miá hábá máunai, bí thoibai.
The man (whom) I taught lives at Gáuháti.	(Zaikhô) áng farangnai, bí Gáuhátiáu tháĭŭ.
I have forgotten the story (which) I heard yesterday.	(Zi) khoráng miá khnánai, bí-khô báugàrbai.

As before remarked, participles in Kachári often take the place of relative pronouns; thus the last sentence given above would be more idiomatically rendered, thus—"Miá (khnánai) khorángkhô báugàrbai," *i.e.*, the story (heard) [by me] yesterday, (I) have forgotten.

9.—(Who) is that man? ... Bí (sur) mànsŭí?
(Whose) *dáu* is this? ... Bí (surni) sekhá?
(Whom) did you see? ... Nang (surkhô) nunaí?
(To whom) did you give it?... Nang bíkhô surnŭ hŭnai ?
(From whom) did you get this? Nang bíkhô (surnifrai) man-ńai ?
(Which way) are you going? Nang (båbething) thángnŭ ?
In (what) village do you live? Nang (båbe) gámiáu thádang ?
(What) do you say? ... Nang (má) khithádang ?
(What) is the matter? ... (Má) záadang ?

10.—(This) is my house ... (Bê) ángni nŭ.
(That) water is cold ... (Boi) dŭíá gassú′.
(These) cows are fat ... (Bê) mosaúfrá găfúng.
(Those) goats are thin ... (Boi) burmáfrá hàmnai.
(These) coolies have finished their work. (Bê) khulifrá hábá máukháng-bai.
(Those) men all went away... (Boi) mànsŭífrá boibo tháng-(tra)bai.* (21 A).

11.—(Somebody) is coming... (Surbá) faidang.
(Some) men are idle ... (Khaisè) mànsŭíá alsíá.
(Each man) must do (his own) work. Mànsŭífrá (gágai gágai) hábá máunŭ nánggô.
(Many) boys have gone away Gåthåfur tháng(tra)bai.*
(As many as) work will receive wages. (Zèsè) hábá máŭŭ darmahá mangan.
(How much) rice is in the granary? Bàndàráu (bèsè) mai danga ?
(How many) men worked in the tea-house to-day? Díni sá-nŭáu (sápsè) mànsŭí hábá máunai ?
(How many) rupees a month do you want? Nang dànfrimbo (bèsè) thà-khá mannŭ nàmáiŭ ?

---

* Intensive particle "tra," attached to verbal root, gives the sense of "many," or "all" ("tra," *intensive* particle. 21 A).

(Other) men will come to-morrow.	Gábun (gúbun) mansŭí faigan.
Bring (as much) rice (as) we want.	(Zèsè) mai nánggô (bisè) lábo.
There is (nobody) in the house	Nŭáu (ráubo * gŭiá.)
{ He does (not) understand (anything). / He understands (nothing) }	Bí (múngbo * mithiá).

12, 13, 14.—VERBS—Active.

Men (eat) rice ...	Mànsŭífur mikhàm (záĭŭ).
Cows (give) milk ...	Mossaúfrá gákhir (hŭĭŭ).
Bears (live) in the jungle ...	Mafúrfrá hágráiáu (tháĭŭ).
The (sun) rises every day ...	Sáná sánfrimbo (ankhárŭ).
They (are cutting) the paddy.	Bísur mai (hádang).
The women (are sifting) rice..	Hinzháusáfur mai (záudang).
He (is building) a house	Bí nŭ (ludang).
The rain (is falling) heavily..	Akhá zábráhŭi (hádang).
I (was going) home when you met me.	Nang ángkhô lagŭ manbá áng nŭáu (thángdangman).
They (were eating) their rice when I came.	Áng faibá bísur mikhàm (zábai thádangman.)
He (was sleeping) when I went out.	Áng baizzháu thángbá bí (udúbai thádangman).
He (has gone) to Gáuháti...	Bí Gáuhátiáu (thángbai).
The paddy (has ripened) ...	Mai (manbai).
The steamer (has reached) Dibrugarh.	Jáházá Dibrugarh (manbai).
They (have forgotten) what I told them.	Áng bisurnŭ khithánai khorángkhô bísur (báugàrbai).

* { "Ráu-bo" / "Múng-bo" } combined with *negative* verb { nobody, no one. / nothing.

He (went) to Mangaldai yesterday.	Bí miá Mangaldŭiáu (tháng-bai).
They (came) to Tezpur last week.	Bísur thángnai hapthásiáu Tezpuráu (faibai).
The wind (blew) strongly all night.	Horsè màni bàr (bàrsŭnai).*
You (cut down) the tree three days ago.	Nang bangfàng (dànnaiá) sám thàm thángbai.
He (had gone out) when I came in.	Áng faibá bí (thángdangman).
You (had written) the letter before I went away.	Áng thángnai áglánŭ nang sithi (lítdangman)
I (had cut) my paddy before you arrived.	Nang fainai áglánŭ áng mai (hádangman).
He (had ploughed) his field before he went home.	Bí nŭáu thángnai áglánŭ dubliáu (háloi oidangman).
I (will bring) thatch to-day...	Díni áng thorŭí (lábogan).
To-morrow I (will build) my granary.	Gábun áng bàndàr (lugan).
Next week I (shall cut) my paddy.	Fainai hapthásiáu áng mai (hágan).
Then I (shall give) my friends a feast.	Abá áng khurmáfurnŭ bhazŭ (hŭgan).
He (will come very soon) ...	Bí (mámàr faisigan).
The paddy (will ripen almost at once).	Maiá dá (mansigan.)
(Go) to school every day ...	Sànfrimbo iskuláu (tháng).
(Honour) your father and mother.	Nangni nammá namfákhô (mainya khlám).
(Love) your enemies ...	Hathrufurkhô (an).
(Let) all men (fear) God ...	Boibo mànsŭífrá Iswarkhô (gíthang).

* "Bàr-sŭ-nai :" "bàr-nŭ," to blow ; "sŭ," intensive affix to verbal root=strongly, heavily, &c. (21 A.)

(If you work) well, you will be rewarded.	Nang gahàm (hábá khàmbá) furuskar mangan.
(If you see) him, call him ...	Bíkhô (nubá) ling.
(Should I meet) him, I shall like him.	Bíkhô (lagŭ manbá), gahàm mangan.
(Had I met) him, I should have liked him.	Bíkhô (lagŭ manbá), gahàm mangaúman.
I (can write) a letter ...	Áng sithi (lítnŭ hágaú).
He was blind, but (can now see).	Bí khànáman* dá (nainŭ hágaú).
I (could do) my work ...	Áng hábá (khàmnŭ hábai).
I (might have loved) him once.	Áng bíkhô khansè (annŭ hábai).
I (shall be able) to do my work.	Áng hábá khàmnŭ (hágan).
They went (to plough) the field.	Dubliáu (háli oinŭ) thángbai.
He goes (to look for) the fowls.	Dáufurkhô (nàmainŭ) thángŭ.
She went (to meet) her brother.	Bí bifangkhô lagŭ lánŭ thángbai.
(Seeing) a tiger, I ran away	Mosákhô (nunánoi) áng khát′-lángnai″sŭí.
(Descending) from a tree, a bear seized him.	Bangfángnifrai (ankhátbánŭ) mafurá bíkhô hambai.
(Having gone) to the house, I saw my friend.	Nŭáu (thángbánŭ) khurmá-khô núnaisŭí.
(Having planted) my rice, I can now rest a little.	Mai (gai′khàngnai″khai) áng dá bángai ziránŭ hágaú.
The (reapers) are in the field	(Mái hánaifra†) dubliáu danga.

* "Khàná-man," for "khàná [A.] daugman," was blind—verbal root omitted and temporal affix only retained. (15 B).

† "Há-nai," past participle from "há-nŭ," to cut—used in *active* sense ; "Mai há-nai " [A.—Dhán dôá] = paddy cutter, reaper.

The (beggar) wants some food	(Bibai'gráiá*) bángai zánai basthu námaidang.

15.—Passive Voice.

Mådh (is drunk) by Kacháris	Båråfrá zaú (langŭ).
Fish (are caught) in nets ...	Zê zang ná (hamŭ).
The cow (was eaten) by a by a tiger.	Mosáiá mosaúkhô (zábai)
The boy (had been killed) by a bear.	Mafurá gâthåkhô {åṛthàṭbai / khuṛthàṭbai}†
The paddy (will be cut) to-morrow.	Gábun mai (hágan).
(Let) the child (be brought) here.	Bêáu gâthåkhô (lábo).
If you steal, you (shall be beaten).	Nang sikháudangbá (buzáagan).
I may (be seen) here ...	Ángkhô bêáunŭ (nainŭ hágaú).
If I (had been beaten) I should have run away.	Áng (buzáabá) khát'lánggaú"-man.
The man (killed) by the tiger (was buried) yesterday.	Mosáiá (åṭnai)‡ mànsŭikhô míá (fôpbai).
(Having been taught) by him, I soon learnt to read.	Bízang (salang'nánoi), áng mámàr farhinŭ rangbai.
On account of the darkness I (was not seen).	Khamsi záanáikhai ángkhô (nuákhŭísè).

* "Bi-bai-grái-á," = "Bí," to ask + "bai," affix denoting *continuous, repeated* action, + "grá," agent (*H.*—Wálá) + "á," definite article (3 D.), "i" being inserted euphonically between the last two syllables, one who is always asking, begging, &c.,—a beggar. (19).

† "Åṛ-thàṭ-bai" ("åṛnŭ," to bite + "thàṭnŭ," to kill) .... bit to death
"Khuṛ-thàṭ-bai" ("khuṛnŭ," to claw, tear, &c., + "thàṭnŭ") .... clawed to death } (19).

‡ "Åṭnai," past participle in "nai" (used in *passive* sense), from "åṭnŭ" (åṛnŭ), to bite,—killed by biting.

It will be observed that in all the sentences above given, with one or two exceptions, the English passive verbs are rendered in Kachári by verbs active; *e.g.*, the Kachári equivalent for "the cow was eaten by a tiger," is, when translated *literally*, "the tiger eat the cow." In short, in this as in some other Oriental tongues, the Passive voice is used only very sparingly and infrequently.

16.—Negative Verbs.

He (does not live) in Tezpur	Bí Tezpuráu (tháiá).
I (am not going) home ...	Áng nŭáu (thángá).
You (were not working) when I came.	Áng faibá nang hábá (máuá-khŭíman).
They (had not caught) any fish when I saw them.	Áng bifurkhô nubá másèbo ná (manákhŭíman).
The coolies (did not pluck) leaf to-day.	Khulifurá díni bilai (kháiá-khŭínŭ).
They (cannot dry) the tea to-day.	Díni sá (frànnŭ) háiá).
They (could not do any hoeing) yesterday.	Miá bísur (khodál záunŭ háiá-khŭísè).
If you are idle, I (shall not like) you.	Nang al'siá záabá áng (gahàm maná).
(Do not drink) much mâdh...	Zábráhŭí zaú (dá langsŭ).*
If I am unwell, I (cannot work).	Áng zobrá záabá (hábá máunŭ háiá).
Because I was unwell, I (could not work).	Zobrá záanaikhai áng (hábá máunŭ háiákhŭísè).
I (shall not come) if it rains...	Akhá hábá áng (faiá).
Being very busy, (I cannot go) to see you.	Ánghá hábá thásŭnaikhai* nangkhô nainŭ (thángnŭ háiá).

* "Sŭ," *intensive* particle, strengthens sense of verbal root. (21).

(Not having finished the work) the sáhib blamed me.	(Hábá máukhàngikhai)† sáhibá ángkhô dai hŭbai.
(Not having) a gun, I could not shoot the tiger.	Ánghá silai (gŭíikhai)‡ mosá-khô gáuthàṭnŭ háiákhŭísè.
(Unless it rains), we cannot do our ploughing.	(Akhá háiábá) zangfur háloi oinŭ háiá.
Come back (without delay) ...	(Gabáu khàmálábá)‖ faifáfin.
(Without diligence) it is impossible to get learning.	(Man hŭálábá)‖ gyán mannŭ háiá.

17.—Causative Verbs, &c.

I (feed) the boys with rice ...	Gâthâfurkhô mikhàm (záhŭ-dang).
He is (shaking) the tree ...	Bangfàngkhô (simáudang).
You (sent) the woman to Gáu-háti.	Nang hingzháusákhô Gáu-hátiáu (haṭbai).
I (was teaching) him to read when you came.	Nang faibá áng bíkhô (farang′-dangman).
They (will dry) the tea in the sun.	Sándungáu sákhô (fràngan).
(Bathe) the child in the river	Gâthâkhô dŭísáiáu (thukhúi).
If you are idle, I (shall have you beaten).	Nang alsiá záabá áng (nangkhô búhŭgan).
If he (had made me learn to read) it would have been well for me.	Bí (ángkhô farangbá) ángnŭ lági gahàm záagaúman.

† "Máu-khàng-i-khai" ("máu-nŭ," to work; "khàng," particle of *completion* (21); "i = á," *negative* particle (16 B.); "khai" [*A.*—Káran] (word denoting relation between cause and effect), "on account of not having finished the work."

‡ "Gŭí-i-khai," substantive verb negative (22 A.) with particle of causation ("khai") attached ("gŭi" = "gŭiá").

‖ "Gabáu khàm-á-lábá" ("khàmnŭ," to do; "á," negative particle; "lábá," adverbial particle) [*A.*--Palam na karákoi] (16 B.); "Man hŭálábá" [*A.*—Man ni diákoi].

He cannot (show) me the horse	Bí ángnŭ goráikhô (naihŭnŭ) háiá.
I (caused) the coolies (to finish) the work yesterday.	Miá khulifurkhô (hábá máukhàng hŭbai).
They could not come (because it rained).	(Akhá hánaikhai) bísur fainŭ háiákhŭísè.
They could come (because it did not rain).	(Akhá háĭkhai *) bísur fainŭ hábai.
(As I did not meet) him, I soon came back.	(Bíkhô lagŭ manikhai*) áng mámàr faifinbai.
I like him, and (therefore) I will live with him.	Áng bíkhô gahàm manŭ, (bíni khai) áng bízang thágan.
You must not (fire) the jungle near the house.	Nŭ khàthini hágráiáu nang (åt lagainŭ) maná.
(Show) me the way to Bengbári.	Bengbáriáu thángnai † námá ángnŭ (dithinánoi hŭ).
(Let me know) all that you saw yesterday.	Nang miá nunai boibo khorángkhô (ángnŭ khĭthá).

18, 19, 20, 21.—Compound Verbs, &c.

Is the water (deep)? No ...	Dŭí (gŭthaú‡) ná? Núngá.
While you (are young), I shall care for you.	Nang (zŭlaúbá§) áng ráhkigan.
When you (are older), you must help me.	Nang (áru boiáh manbá) ángkhô hahai khàmnŭ nánggô.
(If you work hard), it will be well for you; but if you are idle, it will not be well.	(Nang sram khàmsŭbá) nangká gahàm záagan; khintu alsiá záabá, hàmá záagan.

* "Há-ĭ-khai;" "há-nŭ," to rain } "ĭ," negative particle; "khai,"
"Man-ĭ-khai;" "man-nŭ," to get } causative particle.

† "Thángnai," past participle from "thángnŭ," to go [*A.*—Zôá].

‡ "Gŭthaú," for "gŭthaú danga": substantive verb omitted. [*A.*—Páni då ne?]

§ "Zŭlaú-bá," for "zŭlaú záabá": adjective and verb combined; verbal root ("záa," be) omitted. (20).

We must make haste, or (it will be evening) before we reach home.	Zang mámàr thángnŭ nánggô, anthaibá zangfurni nŭ maná sáunŭ * (manágan †).
(It is getting dark) even now.	Dábo (bángai khamsi záanŭ nàmaidang.
The sun is rising, and it will soon (be light).	Sán ankhàtdang, áru mámàr (sránggan †).
We must reach Orang (before evening comes on).	(Manáiá sáunŭ *) zangfur Orang mannŭ nánggô.
(When I am rich), I will give you some books.	(Áng sohoki záabá) nangnŭ khitáp hŭgan.
He (was very strong), and therefore could do his work very easily.	Bí (balágrá khai ‡) gágaini hábá găthai gallŭíhènŭ khàmnŭ hábai.
It was (dark night) when he arrived.	Bí fainaiáu (hor khamsi §) man. ‖
I (have eaten) my rice ...	Áng mikhàm (zábai).

---

* "Man-á sáunŭ" ("man," root of "mannŭ," to get, reach; "á," negative affix; "sáu," over, before; "nŭ," enclitic of emphasis)= before we reach; before reaching.

"Maná-i-á," for "maná zaaiá," verbal root omitted (20); "sáunŭ," over, before. "Maná," evening; "i," euphonic affix combining with preceding vowel to form diphthong "ái" (3 C. D.); "á" negative affix. Preposition, "sáu," over, preceded by a negative verb, gives the sense of "before," &c.

† "Manágan"; "maná," evening } + "gan" = "záagan" (20) } will be { evening.
"Sránggan," "sráng," light } + "gan" = "záagan" (20) } will be { light.

‡ "Balágrá-khai," for "balágrá záanai khai" (20), through being strong.

§ "Hor khamsi," *lit.*, night dark ("pitch dark"); "hor" (night), used in adjectival sense (="hor-ni khamsi," darkness of night.)

‖ "Man," for "dangman" (was) (15 B.); substantive verb combined with noun. (20.)

I have (quite finished eating) my rice.	Áng mikhàm (zákhàngbai *).
This horse (can run) ...	Bê goráiá (khàtnŭ hágaú).
That horse (ran away altogether).	Boi goráiá (găthainŭ khàtlángbai *).
Birds (fly) in the air ...	Dáufrá bàráu (bírbáĭŭ ‡).
My little bird (flew away) yesterday.	Ángni dáu udúĭá míá (bírlángbai *)
The jungle (is burning) ...	Hágrá (khàmdang).
The jungle (has been quite burnt up).	Hágrá (khàmtrabai *).
The water is deep, and your *dhuti*—loincloth—(will be wetted).	Dŭí găthaú, nangni gàmsá (sígan).
The river was very deep, and my *dhuti* (was quite wet through).	Dŭísá găthaúsin áru ángni gàmsá (găthai sítrabai *).
Kacháris (like) mâdh ...	Bârâfrá zaú (găhàm manŭ).
That sot (will drink up) all the mâdh.	Boi fêgráiá zaú gasŭínŭkhôbo (langtragan *).
I (saw) a snake here last week	Thángnai haftaiáu áng beaúnŭ zibaú másè (nunai).
In this village there (are many snakes).	Bê gámiáu zibaú (dangsŭïa †).
I (begged) him to help me ...	Ángkhô hohai khàmnŭ (bíbai).
This man is always (begging)	Bê mànsŭíá azainŭ (bí'baibá"ĭŭ ‡).

* "Khàng," "láng," "tra," &c., intensive particles giving the sense of *completeness* to the action denoted by preceding verbal root. (20 A).

† "Dang-sŭ-ĭ-a" ("dang," substantive verb, 15 B.; "sŭ," intensive particle = many; "ĭ," euphonic affix; "a," terminal affix) = "there are many."

‡ "Bír-bá-ĭ-ŭ" ("bírnŭ," to fly, + "bai," affix expressive of *continuous* progressive action) = "keep flying about." *Cf.* "Bínŭ," to beg; "bi-bai-grá," one who begs continuously,—a professional beggar. (19).

I (shall cut) my paddy next month.	Fainai dànsiáu ángni (maikhô hágan).
The people of that village (finished cutting) their paddy last week.	Boi gámini mànsŭífrá tháng-nai haftásiáu mai (hákhàng-bai *).
I (struck the dog and killed) it	Áng (sŭímákhô buthàṛbai †).
Dogs (wander about) the town	Sŭimáfrá nagaráu (thàbai'bai-thá''ïu ‡).

22.—Defective and Auxiliary Verbs.

Is this your goat? (No) ...	Bê nangni burmá´ ná ?§ (Núngá §).
It (was) mine, but it is now his.	Áng ni (man ‖), dá bíni.
There (is not) one cow in the village.	Gámiáu másèbo mosaú (gŭíá).
(Is there) any rice in the house? No.	Nŭáu bángái mairang (danga ná)? Gŭíá.
(If there are no) fowls, I cannot get my dinner.	Dáu (gŭíábá ¶), áng mikhàm man-nŭ háiá.
You have brought the fire-wood, (have you not)?	Nang ban lábobai, (núngá ná §)?

* "Khàng," "lang," "tra," &c., intensive particles giving the sense of *completeness* to the action denoted by preceding verbal root. (20 A).

† "Bu-thàṛ-bai" ("búnŭ," to strike, + "thàṛnŭ," to kill), to kill by striking. (19).

‡ "Bír-bá-ï-ŭ" ("bírnŭ," to fly, + "bai," affix expressive of *continuous* progressive action)="keep flying about." *Cf.* "Bínŭ," to beg; "bi-bai-grá," one who begs continuously,—a professional beggar. (19).

§ "Ná," used of simple interrogation.

"Núngá ná," used where an *affirmative* answer is implied. [*A.*—Na hoi ne?]

‖ "Man=dangman," was. (15 B.)

¶ "Negative verb "gŭíá," in subjunctive mood. (22 A. B.)

You (must not drink) dirty water; if you do, you may get cholera.	Nang gázri dŭí (langnŭ maná); langbá, máŭr hamnŭ hágaú.
Men (must not quarrel): they (ought to love each other).	Mànsŭífrá (nángzlainŭ* maná): bísurá (anzlainaiá* gŭhàm).
All men (must do) their duty	Boibo mànsŭífrá máunŭ gnáng † hábákhô (máunŭ nánggô).
You (must go) to Orang to-day: come back without delay.	Díni nang Orangáu (thángnŭ nánggô): găbáu khàmá lábá faifin.
We (must) sometimes give up our rights, so that there may not be a quarrel among us.	Zangfur mobábá mobábá mannŭ gnángkhôbo † gàrnŭ (nánggô), mánathŭ zangfurni gezráu bibád záaiá zásè.
(Under the circumstances), I cannot give you anything.	(Erŭíbá ‡) áng nangnŭ múngbo hŭnŭ háiá.
There is (not even a single) pig in this village.	Bê gámiáunŭ omá másè gŭíliá §).

---

* "Náng-zlai-nŭ:" "náng-nŭ," to fight } + "zlai," particle denoting
"An-zlai-nŭ:" "an-nŭ," to love } RECIPROCAL action.

"An-zlai-nai-á;" past part. used in *active* sense [*A.*—Íte híte prem kará], equivalent to a verbal noun; *lit.*, "(Their) loving each other is good." (19).

† Máu-nŭ gnáng hábá } "What (men) { do,"—duty } (22 B.)
Man-nŭ gnáng } ought to { get,"—rights }

Verbal nouns compounded with the particle of obligation, &c., "gnáng."

‡ "Erŭí-bá:" "erŭí," thus + "bá" (for "záabá"), if it be; *lit.*, if it be thus [*A.*—Ene hole; or, Ene hoi zadi]. Subjunctive mood of the substantive verb "záanŭ" compounded with the adverb "erŭí," thus. (20 B.)

§ "Gŭí-li-á," strongly emphatic form of negative substantive verb "gŭiá." (22 B.)

23.—INDECLINABLE WORDS.—ADVERBS, &c.

(Where) are you going? ...	Nang (mohá) thángnŭ?*
(When) did the syce come?	Sois (mobá) {faibai? / faikhŭ?}
(How) can I see in the night-time?	Horáu (mábrŭí) nunŭ?*
You must come back (quickly)	Nang (mámàr) faifinnŭ nánggô.
(How very slowly and badly) the men are working (to-day).	(Díni) mànsŭífrá (mábrŭí làsè áru hàmè) hábá máudang.
Can the horse canter (well)?	Goráiá (gàhàmŭí) khàtnŭ hágaú ná?
Tell the coolies to hoe (deeply)	Khulifurkhô (gathaúhŭí) záunŭ khíthá.
The rain fell (heavily) last night.	Thángnaĭ horáu akhá há(sŭ)-bai.†
The leaf is coming out (in great quantities).	Bilai (zábráhŭí) ankhàtdang
Dry the tea (slowly and carefully).	(Làsè áru háwadhánhŭí) sá bilai fràn.
My head pains me (greatly)	Khârâ sá(sŭ)dang.†
Take some medicine (at once).	(Dánŭ) bángai mulikhô zá.
Try to sleep (soundly) ...	(Gàhàmhŭí) udúnŭ uphai klàm.
They came to Tezpur (altogether), but the boy went back (alone).	Bísur (lagŭsè) Tezpuráu faibai, khintu gâtháá (hátsinghŭí) thángfinbai.

* "Tháng-nŭ" } "Nu-nŭ" ... } Infinitives used elliptically with force of Indicative Mood in Interrogative sentences. (14 B).

† "Sá-sŭ-dang,"—"sá-nŭ," to be in pain } "Há-sŭ-bai,"—"há-nŭ," to rain ...... } + "sŭ," intensive particle. (21 A).

There were (only) three men in the house (when) I came	Áng fai(bá), nüáu sáthàm màn-süí (bålå) dangman.
The coolie was ill (yesterday), but is well again (to-day).	(Míá) khuliá lam záadangman khinthu (díni) gàhàm záadang.
I cannot come (to-morrow), though I may (on the day after).	(Gábun) fainü háiá, khinthu (sapnehá fainü) hágaú, dáng.*
(Although) we break God's law, He loves us.	Iswarni bidhàn sefai (bábü †), Bí zangfurkhô anü.

24, 25, 26.—PREPOSITIONS, CONJUNCTIONS, &c.

Come (into) the house (with) me.	Áng (zang) nü sing(áu) fai.
Are you going (as far as) Tezpur?	Nang Tezpur (há lági) tháng-nü‡ ná?
Put the saddle (on) the horse.	Goráini (sáiáu) zim khá.
Do not sit (under) a tree when it is lightening.	Akhá mablípbá bangfàngni (singáu) dá zü.
Walk on (before) me ...	Ángni (sïgáng) thàbai láng.
Go home (before) it gets dark	Khamsi záaiá (sáunü) nüiáu tháng.
He is ploughing (in the middle) of the field.	Dubli (gezráu) bí háloi oidang.

* "Dáng" [A.—Hobolá, perhaps, may be], adverb used independently at end of sentences.

† "Bá-bü" [A.—Zadio, although, even if], always used as *affix* to the verb.

‡ "Tháng-nü," Infinitive used interrogatively as an Indicative. (14 B).

English	Kachári
Take two rupees (from) the man and give them (to) the boy.	Mànsŭí(nifrai) thàkhá thainŭí lánánoi * gåthå(nŭ)hŭ.
Light the fire (and) prepare dinner.	Åt su(nánoi *) mikhàm sang.
It rained heavily; (therefore) I could not come.	Akhá hásŭnai * (khai) áng fainŭ háiákhŭísè.
This cloth is (neither) white (nor) black.	Bê hiá gŭfút(bo núngá), gŭsam(bo núngá)
If you work well, you shall be rewarded.	Nang gahàmhŭí hábá máu(bá), bakhshish mangan.
I shall praise you (if) you are good; (otherwise), I shall not like you.	Nang gahàm(bá) áng nangkhô prasansá khàmgan; (núngábá †), áng gahám maná.
I shot at the tiger (and killed it).	Áng mosákhô gáu(thàṭbai ‡).
(O) Sir, I am starving; give me a little food.	(Hai) sáhib, áng ukhú'īnánoi thoinŭ nàmaidang; ángnŭ bángai mikhàm hŭ.
(Look there!) the coolies are striking each other.	(Håånoi!) khulifrá buzlaidang.‖

---

* "Lá-ná-noi," "sunánoi," "Há-sŭ-nai-khai," } participles used instead of conjunctions (25).

† "Núng-á-bá," subjunctive mood of negative verb, "núngá" (22 A), If (you) are not (good), *i.e.*, otherwise.

‡ "Gáu-thàṭ-bai;" force of the *two* verbs "shot" and "killed" expressed by the compound verb, "gáu-thàṭ-bai" [*A.*—Gúliai márilô*n*], *i.e.*, "shot at with fatal effect." (19.)

‖ "Bu-zlai-dang:" "bu," beat, + "zlaí," particle denoting reflexive, reciprocal action. (19 C).

MISCELLANEOUS PHRASES.

I.—Travel.

How far is it from Tezpur to Orang?	Tezpurnifrai Oranghá lági bèsè gŭzàn?
It will be hard to get there in one day.	Sánsèáu bíkhô manhŭínŭ † thán * záagan.
You will want three or four horses to do it.	Bíkhô khàmnŭ máthàm mábrŭí gorai nánggan.
Is the road good? ...	Áli lámáiá gahàm ná?
Yes, but the bridges are bad...	Núnggô, khintu dalengfrá hàmá.
You will have to cross three or four (unbridged) rivers.	(Daleng gŭíë ‡) dŭísákhô manthàm manbrŭí bátnŭ nánggan.
Are there any rest-houses on the way?	Lama khàthiáu dak nŭ dang ná gŭíá?
Yes, three or four ...	Núnggô, gangtham gangbrŭí danga.
Is there danger of seeing bears or tigers on the road?	Lámáiáu thangniáu § mafur bá mosákhô ankhàṭnai gínŭ nanggô na nanga.
Not in the day-time, but they sometimes come out at night.	Sanau gínŭ nángá, khintu horáu mobábá mobábá ankhárŭ.

---

* "Thán" [A.—Ṭán]; "háthi" [A.—Háti]. In words borrowed from other languages, the Kacháris often substitute an aspirated consonant for an unaspirated one at the beginning of a word or syllable; *e.g.*, "kintu," becomes "khintu," &c. (27 A).

† "Manhŭínŭ,"—"man-hŭí-nŭ" = [*A.*—Pábogoi], to reach a place in travelling.

‡ "Daleng gŭíë,"—"daleng," bridge + "gŭíë," (for "gŭíá,") negative verbal particle (22 A), bridgeless [*A.*—Daleng nai kiá].

§ "Tháng-ni-áu," present participle in locative case, "in going

I shall want two elephants for my baggage.	Basthunu lági háthi * manui nánggan.
If there are no elephants, tell the mouzádár to send coolies.	Háthi * guiábá khulifurkhô haṭnŭ mouzáhdárnŭ khĭthá.
I can get you twenty coolies to-morrow ; but you must pay them four annas a day.	Gábun nangnŭ lági ekhuri khulifrá hŭnŭ hágaú, khintu bisurnŭ nang sánfrimbo † hikifá † hikifá hŭnŭ nánggô.
Can I get supplies easily at Orang ?	Orangau áng gár'laihuí rasad mannŭ hágaú ná ?
Yes, but you must give notice of your coming beforehand.	Núnggô, khintu nang fainai áglánŭ bátrá hŭnŭ nánggô.
What is the price of ducks there ?	Boiáu ‡ hángsŭni dorá bèsè ?
How many fowls can be bought for a rupee ? Five or six.	Thàkhá thaisèáu bese dau bainŭ hágaú ? Mábá bá márŭ.
Tell the mouzahdar to collect some firewood and *dhán* for the horses.	Mouzáhdárnŭ khĭthá bángai ban áru gorainŭ lági mai lábothang.
Dhán is very cheap,—only 10 annas a maund.	Maini dorá khâm §; monfáiáu áná zŭ bâlâ.

* "Thán" [*A.*—Ṭán]; "háthi" [*A.*—Háti]. In words borrowed from other languages, the Kacháris often substitute an aspirated consonant for an unaspirated one at the beginning of a word or syllable : *e.g.*, "kintu," become "khintu," &c. (27 A).

† "Sán-frim-bo,"—"sán," (1) sun ; (2) day + "frim" } *distributive* particles { *each* day.
"Hikifá,"—"hiki" [*A.*—Siki] 4 annas + "fá" } *distributive* particles { 4 annas *each*.

"Boiáu," / "Biáu," } there ; used of comparatively { *near* objects. / *remote* distances.

"Khâm ;" [*A.*—Kam]
"Khintu ;" [*A.*—Kintu]
"Kháran ;" [*A.*—Káran]
"Fungzáni ;" [*A.*—Púá]
} the unaspirated initial consonant being changed into an aspirated one.

Can good water be obtained near the bungalow?	Bangláni khathiau duí gŭhám mangaú ná?
Yes, there is a river close at hand.	Núnggô, gŭthai′ khàthiáunŭ dŭísá danga.
Tell the mandals and gáon-burhás to meet me at the bungalow early in the morning.	Bangláiáu fungzáni* ángkhô lagŭ mannŭ mandal áru gàmbráfurnŭ khĭthá.
What kind of people live in this mouzah,—Kacháris or Hindus?	Bê mouzáiáu má mànsŭíá tháiŭ; Bårå bá Hàrsá.†
Some are Kacháris, some Hindus.	Khaisè Bårå, khaisè Hàrsá.
Can I get any salt or sugar at the shop?	Dakhánáu bángai sangkhrŭí bá gúrdŭí ‡ mannŭ hagau na?
Yes, but there are no potatoes	Núnggô, khintu * thá gma.
Call me early, for I must march to Událgúri to-morrow.	Fungzáni ángkhô ling; kháran * gábun Událgúriáu thángnŭ nánggan.

II.—Conversation with a Mouzáhdár.

Are the rice-crops doing well in your mouzáh?	Nangni mouzáiáu mai gahám-hŭí ankhàtdang ná?
Yes, Sir, but we want more rain.	Núnggô, sáheb, khintu akhá zábráhŭí nánggô.
You should make water-channels, and bring water from the rivers.	Nang danggå záunánoi dŭís-ánifrai dŭí lábonŭ nánggô.

* "Khâm;" [*A.*—Kam]
"Khintu;" [*A.*—Kintu]
"Kháran;" [*A.*—Káran]
"Fungzáni;" [*A.*—Púá]
} the unaspirated initial consonant being changed into an aspirated one.

† "Hàr-sá," the word used by Kacháris to designate *all* foreigners and outsiders; a non-Kachári (=" Gentile," "Barbarian, &c.")

‡ "Gúrdŭí;" "gúr" [*A.*—Molasses] + "dŭí," water; molasses-water. *Cf.* "Dáu dŭí" (*lit.*, "fowl's water"), egg.

We Kacháris of the Duárs always do that.	Zang Duáráu thánai Bårâfrá azainŭ bibaidi khàmŭ.
Have you got in the revenue for this year?	Bê basarni kházana nang zâkhàmnai ná?
I have collected more than one-half, but not all.	Kháusènŭkhri zábrá zâkhám-bai; khintu gasênŭkhôbŭ zâkhàm'ákhŭí.
Have you repaired all your roads and bridges?	Nangni boibo áli áru da'leng-fur''khô thik khámbai ná?
The roads are in good order, but it is difficult to get timber for the bridges.	Álifrá gahámhŭí danga, khintu dalengfránŭ lági bangfàng mannŭ gŭíá.
You must always put your roads in order before December; then the ryots will have time to cut their rice.	Disimbar mángsŭni áglánŭ nangni álifurkhô gahàm khàmnŭ nánggô; bibai diblá* raiatfrá mai hánŭ far† mangan.
I hope there is no cholera or small-pox in your mouzah.	Nangni mouzáiáu máŭr bá ai-birám gŭíá hannŭnoi ákhá‡ khàmdang.
There have been a few cases of cholera, but there are none now.	Máŭr surhábá‖ surhábá záa-dangman, khintu dá gŭíá.

* "Bibaidi-blá:" "bibaidi," thus, so; "blá" (for "záablá"), subjunctive mood from "záanŭ," to be; "if it be so," *i.e.*, then.

† "Far" [*A.*—Pâr] = "samoi;" time, leisure, opportunity, &c.

‡ "Ákhá" [*A.*—Ásá, hope], the guttural aspirate "kh" taking the place of the sibilant "s," a rule to which there are few, if any, exceptions in words borrowed from other languages by Kacháris. (27 D.)

‖ "Sur-há-bá," possessive case of adjective pronoun, "surbá," compounded from "sur" [*A.*—Kôn] and "bá," *indefinite* particle [*A.*—Kônôbá.]

N.B.—The case-ending "há," is attached directly to the radical part of the word and placed *before* the *indefinite* qualifying particle, "bá."

Tell your people not to eat unripe fruit.	Nangni mànsŭífurnŭ khĭthá, fithai gŭtháng dá záthang.
Be very careful not to let them drink dirty water.	Háwadhán khàmnánoi bisurkho gázri dŭí langnŭ dá hŭ.
They must not take drinking-water from the tank in which they bathe.	Bisur dugú'ĭnai pukhrinifrai langnai dŭí lángnŭ maná.*
Make them keep their homesteads clean and free from jungle.	Bisurni nŭni khàthiáu thánai mozáng áru hágrái gŭíĕ † rákhinŭ hŭ.
Are there many opium-eaters in this mouzah ?	Bê mouzáiáu kháni zánai mànsŭí dangsŭía ‡ ná ?
Only a few ; the Kacháris do not eat much opium : they drink mådh and *photiká*.	Bángai bålå danga ; Båråfrá găbáng kháni záiá : bísur zaú fithikhásŭ ‖ langŭ.
A little mådh is good sometimes ; but the Kacháris drink too much.	Mobábá mobábá bángai zaú langnai gahàm ; khintu Bårâfra zabránŭ langŭ.
They do not drink much in their own villages ; they drink when they meet their friends at the market.	Gágaini gámiáu thábá gabáng zaú langá ; háthâu khúrmáfurkhô lagŭ manbá zábráhŭí langŭ.
It would be a good thing, if there were no liquor-shops near the market-place.	Háthŭni kháthiáu zaú fànnai dakhán gŭíábá gahám.

* "Man-á," negative form of "mannŭ," with ethical sense [*A.*—Na pai], "ought not."

† "Hagra gŭíĕ :" "hágrá," jungle + "gŭíá," negative verb, the final syllable of the latter word being slightly changed in composition. (22A.)

‡ "Dang-sŭ-í-a," root of the substantive verb, "dang" (is, are) followed by intensive particle, "sŭ," with the final letter of which the euphonic "í" is combined, forming the diphthong "ŭí."

‖ "Fithikhá-sŭ :" "sŭ," euphonic enclitic, here almost = "and" [*A.*—Mådh photiká-o, madh *and* photiká].

Then we should not find so much drunkenness as we now do.	Boibai'diblá, díni zèsè fêdang, abá bisè fênai mànsŭífurkhô manglágaúman.*
Is there any tea-factory in your mouzáh ?	Nangni mouzáiáu sá bári danga ná ?
Yes ; there is a large one about three miles to the north.	Núnggô; sáf àtsúi mail thàmáu† sá bári gangsè gădít dang.
Some of my ryots go there to work ; else they could not pay their rent.	Ángni raiatfrá khaisè boiáu hábá máunŭ thángŭ ; bibaidi núngábá, bísur kházana hŭnŭ háiá.

III.—Tea-factory Talk with Kachári Labourers, &c.

Why do you come to my garden ?	Nangsur ángni bághisáu mánŭ faidang ?
We come to look for work, sir.	Sáhib, zangfur hábá nàmainŭ faidang.
Are you willing to stay on my garden for the whole year ?	Basarsè ángni bághisáu nangsur thánŭ nàmaiŭ ná ?
Yes, sir, if you will let us do "doubles" sometimes.	Núnggô, sáheb, zangfurnŭ mobábá mobábá dabal khàmnŭ hŭbá.
How much do you want a month ?	Dànfrimbo bèsè mannŭ nàmaiŭ ?
Five rupees, with *bakhshish* now and then.	Thaibá, áru mobábá mobábá bakhshish hŭgan.
Will you give me an agreement if I give you an advance ?	Áng nangsurnŭ haulat hŭbá nangsur ángnŭ agrímint hŭgan ná ?
We will give an agreement for one year only.	Basarsèni bàlà agrímint hŭgan.

* "Man-glá-gaú-man," past tense subjunctive in *negative* form of the verb, "mannŭ," to get, find, meet with.

† "Thàm-áu," numeral "thàm" (three), with case-ending (locative) attached.

What work have you done to-day?	Díni nangsur má hábá máukhŭ? *
Your hoeing is bad; you must clear the roots of the plants from jungle.	Nangsur kharâï záunaiá † hàmá; bangfàngfurni radánifrai hágrákhô gàrnŭ nánggô.
How many doubles at hoeing have you done this week?	Kharâï záuniáu bê hapthásiáu bèsè dabal khlàmnai?
You will have to roll leaf to-morrow.	Gábun nangsur bilaikhô nánŭ nánggan.
You must go to work earlier in the morning than you did yesterday.	Miánŭkhri fungzamıá nınu habá máunŭ thángnŭ nánggô.
If you roll leaf in the morning, I will allow you a double at the hoe in the afternoon.	Fungzáni bilai nánaibá, áng sánzufuáu ‡ kharâï záuniáu † dabal mansè hŭgan.
You must not merely scrape the ground; but strike the hoe well into the soil, and turn it over.	Nangsur há sannu bâlâ nanga; khintu gahámhŭí záunánoi hákhô fáfinnánoi hŭ.
Why has your wife not gone to pluck leaf to-day?	Nangni hingzháuá díni manu bilai khanu thángákhuí?
Is she not well? Come to the bungalow, and I will give you some medicine for her.	Bíni mâdama § gahàm núngá ná? Bangláiáu fai, áru bínŭ lági áng nangnŭ bángai múli hŭgan.

* "Máu-khŭ," abnormal form of past tense, used in asking questions. (14 B.)

† "Kharâï záu-nai-á," *past* participle used as a verbal noun in *nominative* case. [*A.*—Tomár kodál párá karam]. (14 C.)

"Kharâï záu-ni-áu," *present* participle used as verbal noun in *locative* case; "in hoeing," *i.e.*, at the hoe. (14 C.)

‡ "Sán-zu-fu-áu," locative case of "sánzufu" [*A.*—Dupar bêlit], noon; mid-day.

§ "Mâdam-á," body. *Lit.*, "Is her body not well?" [*A.*—Táir gá bhál na hoi ne?]

Report to me to-morrow, if she is better.	Bíni mådamá gahám bá hàmá, gábun ángnŭ khĭthá.
Some of your children might go out to pluck leaf; they will get two pice a seer.	Nangni gåthåfrá khaisè an-khàṭnánoi bilai khánŭ há-gaú; sêrfáiáu* phoisá gatnè mangan.
If all your family pluck leaf, they will get 15 or 20 rupees a month in a good flush.	Nangni foriál boibo bilai khá-bá, bilai zábrá záablá dàn-fáiáu* pandra bá ekhuri thàkhá mangan.
Some of our children wish to go to school.	Zangfurni gåthåfrá khaisè iskuláu thángnŭ nàmaiŭ.
Very well; I will open a school for them in the cold weather.	Gahám; gazáng bathráu bisur-ni lági iskul fáthigan.
Is there a river near the factory? We Kacháris like to live where we can catch fish for ourselves.	Bághisáni khàthiáu duísa danga na? Zêráu zangfur gágainŭ ná hamnŭ hágaú, zangfur Båråfrá boiáunŭ thánŭ gahàm manŭ.
Yes; there is a river with plenty of fish.	Núnggô; ná thásŭnai† dŭísa danga.
Take care you do not drink too much mådh when you go to the market.	Nangsur háthánu thángbá, man hŭnánoi zábrá zaú dálang.

*{"Sêr-fái-áu:" "sêr" (sír) ... / "Dàn-fái-áu:" "dàn," month} + "fá," distributive particle; + locative case-ending.

N.B.—In both these instances the vowel "i" is euphonically inserted between the distributive particle "fá" and the case-ending "áu," this vowel combining with the preceding "á" to form the diphthong "ái."

† "Ná thá-sŭ-nai" [*A.*—Bahut más thaká], a compound adjective qualifying the noun "dŭísá." "Thá-sŭ-nai," past participle from "thánŭ," to be, remain,—the intensive particle "sŭ" (=many, much) being inserted between the verbal root "thá" and the participial affix "nai." (14 C).

READING LESSONS.

The short series of Reading Lessons given in the following pages, will afford the student some insight into the more prominent characteristics of the language when thrown into the form of continuous narrative. They may be divided into three groups: Nos. 1--8 are translations from a school-book which is highly popular in the Kachári village schools of this district, the "Assamese Second Reader," published at the American Mission Press, Sibságar; Nos. 9—11 are translations of the Creed, the Lord's Prayer, and the Ten Commandments, the texts for translation being taken from the Assamese Version of the Book of Common Prayer; while the third group, which is perhaps the most important, consists of original compositions descriptive of some of the more prominent features of Kachári village life, religious, social, domestic, &c. These last chapters (Nos. 12—17) have for the most part been compiled by J. Dhan Singh, a Kachári native of Sílputá mouzáh, Chátgári Duár, in the Mangaldai sub-division of this (Darrang) district.

The learner should carefully endeavour from the first to distinguish between what is *radical* and *essential* in a word, and what is merely *inflectional* and *formative*. Under this latter head are, of course, comprised the case-endings of nouns, the modal and temporal affixes of verbs, enclitic particles, &c. Thus in the word, "Tháng-ni-áu-nŭ" ("even while going,") each syllable, as it were, makes a distinct contribution to the meaning of the whole word. We have first the radical (root) part of the word, "tháng," go; "ni" is the termination of the present participle, "tháng-ni," going; "áu" is the case-ending (locative) denoting the *time*, *place*, &c., of the act of going—"tháng-ni-áu," in (=when) going; while the last syllable, "nŭ," is a kind of euphonic enclitic, which perhaps serves slightly to strengthen the sense of the whole word, and may conveniently be rendered by "even," or some equivalent term. The learner will find his progress in acquiring a knowledge of Kachári materially aided by constantly endeavouring to analyse all the longer words, and ascertaining how much each *part* of any word contributes towards the meaning of the *whole*: and the compiler has endeavoured to assist him in carrying out this plan in two ways; *viz.*, 1, by separating (by means of a hyphen) the radical from the inflectional part of a word, in the first three or four sections of the Reading Lessons; and 2, by analysing, or otherwise explaining, some of the more difficult words and unusual forms of expression, in foot-notes appended to each lesson. With this assistance and with that of a brief Vocabulary appended to the Lessons, a learner of average ability and fair powers of application ought not to find any insuperable difficulty in mastering the meaning of the Lessons, though the help of an intelligent Kachári (*e.g.*, a mandal or mouzáhdár) may at times be desirable, especially in reading the last six or eight sections.

N.B.—Words adopted from the Assamese, &c., when their form has undergone any material change, are indicated by an [A.] in brackets; but it has not been thought necessary to adopt this practice in all cases, *i.e.*, in words which have been so slightly (if at all) changed, that they can hardly fail to be recognised at once by every average Assamese scholar.

1.—THE SHEEP.

Menda mungbo habá maŭ-á, khintu [A.] bí-ni khaman zang gahàm hí dá-ï-ŭ; bí-ni fĭsá-frá hatbai bai-ŭí bai-ŭí gele-u.

Menda ba bí-ni fĭsa-kho dukhu [A.] dá hŭ, aru bifar-khô âṛ-nŭ lági sŭímá-khô dá thin; mánathŭ bí-sur hazá [A.] ráu-ni-bo múngbo háni khàm-a.

Mai, sabai, gàngsa zanu lági mendà gahàm man-ŭ. Bí-khô sangkhruí hŭ-na-noi gàngsa gahàm-ŭi zá-hŭ-bá, bí gagai-ni gurŭí khaman dáng-nŭ lági hŭ-ï-ŭ.

2.—THE DOG.

Sŭímái-á hor-áu nŭ rákhi-u; bí sikháu nu-blá sang-ŭ; dàn-sráng* záa-bá sang-sŭ-ī-ŭ.†

Sŭímái-á mendà bá masaú-far-khô åṛ-ŭ, árŭ båbebá båbebá sŭímáiá mànsŭí-khô-bo åṛ-ŭ. Bí-khô ikhàm árŭ bidaṭ zá-hŭ-nŭ náng-gô; bí mudú-bai thá-ni-áu,‡ bí-ni átheng bá lànzái-áu dá gá.

Sŭímái-á máu-nu mungbo hába gu-ö khai dukhiá mànsŭí-á zábrá sŭímá fĭsí′-ni-á gahàm núng-á.

3.—THE CAT.

Mauzi inzat bonggá inzat ham-nŭ lagi găhàm. Zang-frá máuzi-khô miú miú hanná-noi ling-ŭ. Máuzi-khô bundŭí zá-nŭ hŭ.

Máuzi-á gúr-gúrai-dang, khná-sang nai. Zeblá bí-há zoḅrá záa-ī-ŭ, abá′niá gúr-gúrai-á.

Máuzi-ni hàthai àsúgur zábrá găfát. Bí-ni khaman árŭ lànzai bú-blá bí khuṛ-ŭ árŭ åṛ-ŭ.

Máuzi-á khamsi-áu-bo nu-ī-ŭ. Hor-áu inzat dal haliá [A.] nàmai-bai-ŭ. Nai-hat nai, boi máuzi-á sŭímái-á ham-gan han-ná-noi gí-ná-noi anthai-ni gorŭ-ni sái-áu uthi-ná-noi thá-dang.

Máuzi-ni khaman guruī aru gudúng naug-u. Zeblá akhá bá gazáng-nai záa-ī-ŭ, abániá bí-khô baizhá lági dá hŭ hat.

---

* "Dàn-sráng" ("dàn," moon, month; "sráng," light), moonlight.

† "Sang-sŭ-ī-ŭ:" "sang-nŭ," to bark; "sŭ," intensive particle—barks much.

‡ "Thá-ni-áu:" pres. part. loc. case, from "thá-nŭ," to remain, continue; in his remaining, *i.e.*, while he remains (asleep).

4.—THE TIGER.

Mosá-ni ubzi-nai [A.] tháuni Asia. Chin árŭ Tatar des-áu-bo mosá man-ŭ, khintu Hindusthàn, Banggàl, Mán árŭ Assàm des-áu zábrá dang-a. Zêr-áu háthi árŭ gàndà tháï-ŭ, boi-áu-nŭ mosái-á-bo tháï-ŭ. Hingha-nŭ-khri mosá-ni bala [A.] bángai khâm, [A.] khintu gubun zanthu-nŭ-khri bí-há bràp-nai gassá; thêö-bo gubun átheng thang-brŭi * zanthu-nŭ-khri bí-khô nai-nŭ mozáng'. Bí-ni baraná fàkhrà sikhrà arthát [A.] fàt-sè găzá, fàt-sè gasam; bí-ni khai mànsui-á bí-khô dinkhiá fátiá han-ŭ Bi ni gada aru udui bángai gufút', båbe-bá båbe-bá mosai-a hingha-ni hamán [A.] găzaú árŭ gălau, khaisè-á bí-ni-khri bo bangai gĭdít dang-a. Iúrop, Amerikà bí-far màni zi zi des-áu mosá thái-á, bí bí des-áu lági fĭsí-nai mosá láng-ná-noi thàkhá man-nŭ áhá-ŭí [A.] gámi gámi thí'thi-bai-bai"-ŭ. Mosái-á sán-áu zábrá-hŭí thábai-á; zeblá ukhŭï-sŭï-ŭ náïbá dŭi gang-ŭ, abá hágrá-ni-frai ankhàr-ná-noi tháng-ná-noi bíla-ni khàthi khàthi mosaú, omá nàmai-báï-ŭ; árŭ mobá-bá mobá-bá mànsui-khô-bo sal-a [A.] nai-ná-noi ham-ná-noi záï-ŭ. Mosai-a mábá-brŭí-bo khan-sè mànsŭí-ni thoi sab-nŭ man-ba, gubun omá-ni thoi bidat-nŭ-khri mansuí-khô găthàu-sin man-ŭ, abániá zeblábá mànsŭí-khô-nŭ nàmai-báï-ŭ.

Mosá bimái-á basar-fái-áu má-thàm má-brŭí erŭíhai fĭsá din-hŭ-ï-ŭ. Árŭ báhá-sè buá fĭsá din'-hŭ-ná-noi-"nŭ mosá bimái-á sàgremá záaï-ŭ han-ná-noi frai [A.] boi-bŭ mànsŭí-frá man fátháï-ŭ árŭ khĭtháï-ŭ.

5.—THE RHINOCEROS.

Gàndà khulu [A.] nè danga; khulusèhá mansè gong, khulusèhá mannè gong, tháïŭ: mansè gong thánai khuluni ubzinai [A.] tháuniá Ásiá, mannè gong thánai khuluákhô

* "Átheng thang-brŭí;" *lit.*, "four feet;" *i.e.*, four-footed animal; quadruped.

Áfrikáu manŭ. Gàndà nainŭ làgi gŭthai gázri, árŭ baranábo bátbini baidi bángai gasam. Bíni mâdamáu khaman gŭíá, khintu bigúrá thai * bar [A.] raza, aru ebrab ebrab khorbla khorbli zaananoi tháīŭ. Athengfrá gusúng, árŭ lànzáiá mudoi, khintu lànzáini bizua guár.

Lànzáini bizúni fàtnèthingbo gărá [A.] khaman tháīŭ. Sáiáuni gushthoiá goráini [A.] saiauni gushthoi baidi; khintu bíni khri gălau árŭ bar gărá. Mábá hamnŭ lági árŭ mobábá bangfàngni dàlaifar safainŭ làgi bí zangnŭ gubun zanthú-nŭkhri bâr sala [A.] manŭ. Singáuni gunthutriá thai,* mosaúni gunthutri baidi. Khâmáiá gĭdít, găfát, árŭ thíá [A.] záanánoi tháīŭ. Bí sesá khâmá baidi khâmá gathang,† bíni khai zániáu náībá [A.] mudúlángniáu mábá'brŭíbá"hŭí· mábá hai [A.] khnábá, abániá gasangnánoi khârâ dikhángnánoi bí haikhô khná'sangnánoi"nŭ‡ hăsú lángŭ.

Mêgan mudoi, ománi mêgan baidi nuīŭ. Mêgan găbáng găzàn gathang† nuē-khai găbáng găzánhá lági nua; bíni sĭgángáu gínai manbá, abá múngbo naia lábá mámàr beg [A.] hŭnánoi hasú lángŭ. Gandaha ganthangni sáiáu zabamni singáu bar gărá gong tháīŭ: bâbebáhá bí gongá mu-sè'-nŭ-khri"-bo gălau, aru bâbebáhá gusúngbo tháīŭ. Gàndàiá bí gongáu bar bala manŭ.

Bâbebá hágráni zanthu [A.] gàndà zang zudha [A.] khàmbá, abá bí bíni ġong zang gágaikhô rákhiŭ [A.] Mosáiá gàndàkhô bala khàmnŭ háiá, háthinŭkhri zábrá gíŭ, mánathŭ gàndàni sĭgángáu thángbá, bí gong zang mosákhô suthárŭ.

---

* "Thai," particle used absolutely [A.—Hole]. "Bigúrá thai," as to its skin: "gunthutriá thai," as regards its lips, &c.

† "Gathang," fully endowed with some physical faculty; *e.g.*—
"Khâmá gathang," quick and keen of hearing.
"Mêgan gathang," quick and keen-sighted.

‡ "Khná'sangnánoi"nŭ" ("khná," to hear; "sang," euphonic affix; "nánoi," conjunctive participle; "nŭ," enclitic), on hearing; when it hears.

Mábá hăsúniáu hágráiáu khàṭlángbá mudoi bangfàngfar manbábo gong zang khundá [A.] márinánoi sefailángŭ. Bíni manàmsŭnai haktiá [A.] sár, bínikhai surbá sikhári [A.] mànsŭífrá bàrbaithing * thángbá bí mámàr manàmnai manŭ; bínikhai sikhárifrá sikhár khàmnŭ thángniáu bíni únfātithing thángŭ; árŭ gàndàfrá mudúlángbá, abá sikháriá sri sri thángnánoi gáutháṛŭ.

Gàndàfrá háthini baidi thafá záanánoi tháĩŭ, mánè másèhŭísŭ tháĩŭ. Árŭ khágrá bárŭí [A.] nalbárŭí [A.] ingkhar bárŭí [A.] bebaidi hágráu bísur tháĩŭ. Mâĩs baidihŭí hábruáu gádoi láĩŭ, árŭ omá baidi hakh-hakh-áĩŭ [A.] Gàndàni bidaṛákhô Bámon [A.] árŭ Hindufrá gathár hannánoi záĩŭ, khintu găbáng găthául núngá: bí gàngsa árŭ bangfàng dàlaifar záĩŭ.

6.—THE CUNNING FISHERMAN.

Sase záluaia [A.] dŭísáiáu zê zang ná guḍbá erŭísŭ mozang másè ná mannaisŭí† ze [A.] bíni baidi ná gubuná manthang sári [A.] ráubo nuákhŭínŭ. Nákhô mannánoi záluáiá manáu [A.] guninaisŭí† ze [A.] bê nákhô hátháu [A.] fànbá bángai thàkhá mangan, khintu rázáni [A.] sĭgángáu lángbá bí nunánoi hanthoh [A.] záanánoi ángkhôbo hanthoh khàmgan. Bêkhônŭ bhábinánoi [A.] záluáiá nákhô lánánoi rázáni sĭgángáu thángnaisŭí.† Nákhô nunánoi rázáiá zábránŭ rangga [A.] mannánoi záluáinŭ abánŭ 100 thàkhá [A.] hŭnŭ ágyá [A.] khlàmnaisŭí.† Biáunŭ manthriá [A.] boi khoráng

---

* "Bàr-bai-thing:" "bàr," wind; "bai," to move, travel; "thing," side, direction; side from which the wind is coming; to windward.

† "Mannai-sŭí," "thángnai-sŭí," &c. In these verbs the last syllable ("sŭí,") seems to affect the sense very slightly, if at all; it may, perhaps, be regarded as a euphonic enclitic, like the syllables "bo" and "nŭ" so frequently used with nouns, pronouns, and adjectives.

khnapanoi hama mannánoi razamau khi'thánai"sŭí,* balŭi,† Másè náiáunŭ 100 thàkhá hŭnaiá usit [A.] núngá. Rázáiá khithánaisŭí,* Áng khansè ágyá khlàmbai, hŭiábá lázi [A.] mangan. Manthriá rázánŭ budi [A.] hŭnaisŭí,* baluí,† Bê náiá zŭ ná zlá bíkhô nangtháng záluainiáu sangthang; zlá hanbá zŭkhô, zŭ hanbá, anthai zlákhô lábonŭ lági záluainŭ ágyá khlàm; árŭ lŭgŭni nákhô lábonánoi hŭnŭ háiábá thàkhá maná záagan, erŭi hannánoi† khithá. Abá rázáiá manthrini budi zangnŭ záluaikhô sangnaisŭí, balŭí.† Bê náiá zŭ ná zlá? Záluaiá khithánaisŭí,* Horgodêo, [A.] bê náiá zlábá núngá zŭbá núngá, bê khásiá [A.] Bê khoráng khnánánoi razaıa mĭníŭí mĭníŭí bínŭ árŭ 100 thàkhá bathá [A.] hŭnaisŭí. Rázáiá áglaiáu 100 thàkhásŭ hŭdangman, khintu manthrini budizang budigrang‡ záluaiá árŭ 100 mannánoi 200 thàkhá kháná lánánoi rangga man zang nŭiáu thángnaisŭí.

7.—THE SECRET OF NEVER-FAILING CHEERFULNESS.

(FROM THE "LARÁR MITTRA.")

Itháli desni [A.] sásè gasaihá [A.] rangga [A.] arŭ hanthoh [A.] záanai swabháo [A.] dangman. Bíni zá'ginai"-

---

* "Mannai-sŭí," "thángnai-sŭí," &c. In these verbs the last syllable ("sŭí,") seems to affect the sense very slightly, if at all; it may, perhaps, be regarded as a euphonic enclitic, like the syllables "bo" and "nŭ" so frequently used with nouns, pronouns, and adjectives.

† "Balŭí." This is the Kachári equivalent (probably the same word) for the Assamese, "buli," and serves to introduce direct narrative or the actual words of a speaker, and may be considered to take the place of inverted commas. Much the same meaning is conveyed by the word, "hannánoi," conjunctive participle of the verb, "hannŭ," to say ("saying.")

‡ "Grang." This word is used much like "gnáng;" *i.e.*, it is combined with nouns to form adjectives; *e.g.*, "Budigrang," possessed of knowledge, shrewd, &c.

ninŭfrai zábránŭ dukhuáu gaglai dangman, khintu bí moblábábo bezàr [A.] mannai záaiáman.*

Bíni bebaidi găhàm swabháo nunánoi, bíni khurma sasea bar ásarit [A.] zaananoi, sànsè bíniáu sangnaisŭí, Heloi, khurmá ! nang ángkhô azainŭ rangga záanaini hankhet [A.] farangnŭ hágaú ná ?

Boiáunŭ boi burai mahazanu [A.] raifinnaisŭi,† balŭí, Áng gŭthai hastháhŭí [A.] angni hankhet farangnŭ hágaú, mánathŭ ángni mêganni ásaran [A.] zang áng azainŭ rangga záabai tháïŭ. Khintu bíni khurmáiá bê khoráng buzi [A.] manikhai,‡ bí erŭí hannánoi sefainánoi khithánaisŭí. Áng zi [A.] awastháiáunŭ [A.] tháïŭ, áglaiá swarga [A.] thing mêgan dikhángnánoi náïŭ, árŭ bhábiŭ [A.] ze bíáu thángnaiásŭ ‖ ánghá beau găhai haba, amphare áng frithibíni [A.] singáu náïŭ, aru bhábiŭ ze áng thoibá bêáu ángnŭ bángai balŭ tháuni nánggan ; ampháre áng frithibíni fàtbrŭíthingbo nainánoi bhábiŭ ze bêáu ángnŭkhribo dukhiá dangsŭia.§ Zeráu erŭíhai thik [A.] hukhu [A.] aru zeráu zangfarni boibo dukhu [A.] árŭ bhábaná [A.] zŭpgan, bíkhọ mithigô. Bínikhai bezar [A.] khlàmnai gŭíá.

---

* "Záaiáman," for "záaiá dangman" [*A.*—No poa ásil].

† "Rai-fin-nai-sŭí :" rainŭ," to speak ; "fin" (faifin), reflexive,—to speak back, to answer.

‡ "Man-i-khai :" "mani," negative form of the verb "mannŭ," to get, obtain ; negative affix "á" giving place to "i." [*A.*—No pôár kárane.]

‖ "Thángnai-á-sŭ :" past part. of verb "thángnŭ," to go, with affix ("á") of nominative case, used as a noun ; "the going ;" "sŭ," enclitic.

§ "Dang-sŭí-a :" substantive verb, "danga," with intensive particle "sŭ" appended, here used *numerically ;* "there are *many* :" "í" affixed to "sŭ" euphonically.

8.—DUTY OF CHILDREN TO THEIR PARENTS.

(From the "Larár Mittra.")

Nangni namfá namákhô an, mánathŭ bísur nangkhô annánoi zá'ginai"nifrai nangkhô frathifálan [A.] khlàmdang. Zeblá nang găthai gălŭí man* árŭ rainŭ bá thábainŭ háiī† gábnánoi bisarkhô dikhàr hŭdangman, ablábo bísar nangkhô frathifál [A.] khlàmbai. Nangnŭ lági namfá namá zerŭí ansŭīŭ, bibaidi árŭ sŭr danga? nangkhô farangnŭ lági bibaidi dukhu sŭr hahidang [A.]? nang zikhini rangdang, bíkhô sŭr farangdang? nangkhô zánŭ árŭ udúnŭ êm banánoi sŭr hŭnai? nangni ranggaáu sŭr rangga manŭ? árŭ nangni dukhuáu sŭr dukhu manŭ? nang lamzáabá‡ sŭr anŭ árŭ frathifálan [A.] khlàmŭ? sŭr nangni găhàm záanŭ Iswarkhô khulúmŭ?

Nangni namfá namákhô maina [A.] khàm. Nangnŭ lági zi găhàm, bíkhô bísur nangnŭ sári zábránŭ mithigô, árŭ bísur nangkhô azainŭ gyáni [A.] árŭ hukhiá [A.] záanŭ lubúīŭ.

Nangni namfá namá lamzáablá‡ bá dukhuáu gaglaibá, bisurkhô hukhiá khlàmnŭ nang zathan [A.] khlàm, árŭ bísur dukhiá záablá frathifálan khlàm. Nangni khai bísur bèsè khlàmdang, árŭ zi dukhu hahidang, bíkhô moblábá dá báugàr.

9.—THE APOSTLES' CREED.

Akhrangsá árŭ frithibi srazigrá boinŭsári balagrásin‖ áfá faram [A.] Iswarákhô áng biswás [A.] khlàmŭ.

---

* "Gălŭí man," for "galŭí dangman," were young, helpless.

† "Hái-ī;" unable, powerless; root, "há" (to be able), with negative affix "i" (for "á"), "i" being inserted euphonically,—a usage of frequent occurrence in Kachári composition.

‡ "Lam-záa-bá;" "lam," fever (ague), with verb "záanŭ," to be, in subjunctive mood, when you had fever ("Lam záanŭ," to have fever.)

‖ "Boinŭ-sári bala-grá-sin:" "boinŭ-sári," than all; "bala" [*A.*—Bal], strength; "grá," agent (possessed of), owner; "sin," sign of superlative degree;—mightier than all; *i.e.*, Almighty.

Árŭ bíni sásè balŭ fīsá zangfarni prabhu Yísu Khrishtakhô, zi fabitra átmánifrai [A.] garbhaiáu hamnai záanánoi, Máriám hingzáusánifrai zágibai, Fantia Filátni ákhúiŭí dukhu bhúg khlàmnánoi, ferengniáu dikhángnánoi záanánoi thoidangman ; árŭ mángkharáu dinnai záadangman, gubun khál hálági thángdangman; sànthàmblá* thoinainifrai uthibai árŭ akhrangsáu lángnai záabai, árŭ boinŭsári balagrásin áfá Iswarni ágdá fàtsi zŭbai thádang ; bínifrai bínŭ thángnai árŭ thoinaifarkhô sangnŭ lági faigan.

Fabitra átmá [A.] ; dharami hádháran mandali [A.]; hádhufarni samanda [A.] ; fáfuni khemá [A.] ; mådåmá fáfin uthinai ; árŭ zŭbi† ziwanákhô áng biswás khlàmŭ.

10.—THE LORD'S PRAYER.

Hê zangfarni akhrangsaiau thanai áfá, nangthángni‡ nau khulúm záanai záathang ; nangthángni raiz [A.] záathang ; zêrehai akhrangsáiáu, êrehai frithibiáubo nangthángni man [A.] fur [A.] záathang ; díni sànáuni ádár zangfarnŭ hu ; árŭ zangfarni dháruáfrákhô zangfar zêrehai ágárŭ, êrehai zangfarnibo dhár hágár ; zangfarkhô farikháiáu [A.] dáláng, khintu dakhnifrai rákhi ; mánathŭ raiz, mahímá [A.] prabháu [A.] bê boibo zebĺábá nangthángni.

11.—THE TEN COMMANDMENTS.

1.—Ángni baizyáu nanghá gubun ráubo Iswar [A.] dá záathang.

---

* "Sàn-thàm-blá," for "sànthàm záablá" ("záanŭ," to be, become), —it having become the third day ; "on the third day."

† "Zŭb-i :" "zŭb-nŭ," to complete, finish, end ; "i" (=á), particle of negation,—unending, eternal.

‡ "Nang-tháng-ni," for "nang-ni ;" "tháng," "honorific" affix,—apparently the only one in the language.

2.—Nang gàgainŭ házinai múngbo múrthi [A.], anthai zi zi basthu [A.] sáu thánai akhrangsauau, anthaiblá singáu thánai frithibíáu, anthaiblá frithibíni singáu thánai dŭíáu danga, bisurni ráunibo múrthi dá khlàm; nang bisurkhô dá khulúm, dá fusibo; mánathŭ nangni Iswar angnŭ manni ad Iswar, manthám manbrŭí furuhá [A.] láginŭ fīsáfarni sáiáu ángkhô mugúīnai bifáfarni adharami fratifal [A.] hŭgrá, árŭ zainŭ ángniáu anŭ,* árŭ ángni aigyá [A.] fáliŭ, [A.] bisurni hàzàr hàzàr [A.] furuhá láginŭ angrá Iswar.

3.—Nangni Iswarni náu eroinu da la, manathŭ zainu bíni náu eroinŭ láīŭ, Prabhuá bíkhô daigŭīī † hannánoi lídá.

4.—Zirainai sàn fabitra bíkhô hunggri. Sànrŭ hábá máunánoi bíni gezráu nanghá boibo hábá khlàm; khintu sànsīníá‡ nangni Iswarni zirainai sàn; bíáu múngbo hábá dá khlàm, nang, anthaibá nangni fīsá, nangni nangsázŭ, nangni bandi, nangni bándi, anthaibá nangni omá,‖ nangni dorni gezráu thánai gubun desni mànsŭí; bê boibo múngbo hábá dá máuthang; mánathŭ Prabhuá akhrangsá árŭ frithibí árŭ hágar, árŭ bíáu zi zifar danga, boikhôbo sànrŭíáu srazibai, árŭ sànsīníáu ziraibai; bíáunŭ Prabhuá zirainai sànákhô bar [A.] hŭnánoi fabitra khlàmbai.

5.—Nang gàgaini namfá namákhô maina [A.] khlàm; bíáunŭ nangni Iswará nangnŭ zi des [A.] hŭīŭ, boi desŭíáu nanghá áīú [A.] gălau záagan.

6.—Nang dá buthàt.

7.—Nang malaini bingzháukhô gaman [A.] dá khlàm.

* "Ángni-áu anŭ;" verb "an-nŭ," to love, governs locative case.

† "Dai-gŭīī:" "dai" [A.], blame; "gŭīī" (for "gŭíá"), negative substantive verb; "blame is not;" blameless. [A.—Dai nai kiá].

‡ "Sànsīní-á:" *ordinal* number denoted by the affix "á" (definite article), "day the seven"—seventh day.

‖ "Omá," pig, hog; here used generically to denote *all* domestic animals, the pig holding so prominent a place in Kachári social and domestic life;—*the* animal, *par excellence*.

8.—Nang sĭkháu dá khlàm.

9.—Nangni gámini ahitŭí [A.] mísá hákhi dá záa.

10.—Nangni gámini nŭĭáu dá lubúï, nangni gámini hing-zháunĭáu, bá bíni bandiáu, bíni bándiáu, bíni masaúáu, bíni goráiáu, bíni múngbo basthuaunu da lubúï.

12.—THE SUN,—SUNRISE, SUNSET, &c.

Sàná modai* hannánoi khitháïŭ. Bíhá gorái danga, boi goráiáu uthinánoi akhrangsá thing thángŭ. Akhrangsáiáu bí thángnai lámá dang, hannánoi khitháïŭ. Bí fungzáni † goráiáu uthinánoi gàgaini lámá thing thángŭí thángŭí‡ sàn-zufuáu ‖ dŭsè § ziráïŭ [A.] Amphárc bínifrai thángnánoi fathál ¶ thing hábhŭïŭ. Abá fatháláu ¶ sàn záahuuu hannánoi khitháïŭ, árŭ bebaidi goraıau uthinánoi gidingbaibai ** tháïŭ hannánoi bungŭ.

13.—PREPARATION OF MÅDH AND PHOTIKÁ.

Zaú sangbá múli hŭ nánggô ; múli hŭíábá †† zaú záaiá. Boi múliákhô thoiár [A.] khlàmnŭ lagi mairang sŭmnánoi

---

* "Modai," any supernatural being, god. [A.—Bhút, dôotá].

† "Fungzáni," in the early morning. [A.—Rátipúá.]

‡ "Thángŭí thángŭí ;" reduplicated particle denotes continuous repeated action. [A.—Goi goi].

‖ "Sànzufuáu," at mid-day.

§ "Dŭ-sè," a little while. [A.—Ek til]. "Dŭsè dá thá," do not stop a moment.

¶ "Fathál-áu," under the earth. [A.—Patál.]

** "Giding-bai-bai :" "giding-nŭ," to go round ; "bainŭ," to con-tinue (in any course of action) : this root being repeated gives the sense of "*continuing* to go round and round time after time."

†† "Hŭí-á-bá :" "hŭ-nŭ," to give ; "á," negative syllable, with "ĭ" inserted euphonically and combining with preceding vowel into diph-thong "ŭí ;" "bá," sign of subjunctive mood ; "if (we) do not give."

dinnŭ nánggô, unáu gurúi záabá makhná bilai árŭ khànthál [A.] bilai zang lŭgŭsè khlàmnánoi saúnŭ nánggô. Amphára gundúi záabá, fithá [A.] baidi ladá khlàmnánoi sàndúngáu rànhŭ * nánggô. Amphára mikhàm sangnánoi, boi emáukhôbo mikhàm gusúng záabá lagainánoi zaúdŭáu sŭnánoi din nánggô. Amphá sànthàm záabá sítnánoi langŭ. Árŭ fithikhá sáunŭbá † dŭí sŭnánoi sànsè bá sànnè din nánggô. Unáu ât zang fudúngnánoi zaúdŭni sáu máthili hŭ nánggô, árŭ máthilini khúgáiáu ôá hàsôngkhô sŭnánoi unthing thingkhiliáu ôá hàsôngkhô sŭ nánggô. Árŭ ukhundŭi thángnŭ háiá zásè ‡ lámáfarkhô lídnŭ nánggô. Árŭ thingkhiliá gudúng záabá sáu dŭí hŭnŭ nánggô. Abánŭ zaúni ukhundŭiá fithikhá záagan.

14.—RELIGION; KACHÁRI DEITIES, &c.

Bàrà mànsŭihá boihábo Bàtthaú modai, Mainán, Khuber, Hásung modai danga. Khaisèhá Hásung modai gŭíá, Bàtthaú bá Sízu modaiánŭ găhai'. Sízu modaiá nŭiáu múngbo záaiá zásè rákhiŭ hannánoi khitháiŭ. Maináuá zánŭ langnŭ thŭhŭiŭ § hanŭ. Khuberá thàkhá [A.] árŭ náná rakam [A.] basthu záhŭiŭ hanŭ. Hásung modaiábo farbáháu ‖ thángbá gahàmŭí

---

* "Ràn-hŭ:" "ràn-nŭ," to dry; "hŭ-nŭ," to give; to give (*i.e.*, to cause) to dry; sign of infinitive ("nŭ") dropped with both verbs, because followed by another verb, "nánggô" (euphonic elision ?)

† "Sáu-nŭ-bá," for "sáu-nŭ záabá," if (we) have to prepare.

‡ "Zásè," conjunction used (always *after* its verb) to express intention *negatively*; "*in order that* it may *not* (be able).

§ "Thŭ-hŭ-ï-ŭ:" "thŭ-nŭ," to suffice; and "hŭ-nŭ," to give; "gives sufficient."

‖ "Farbáhán" [A.—Prabarti], in travelling. "Hásung," god of travellers.

rákhiŭ hanŭ. Bêfar modaini baizzháu hágráni modai zábránŭ danga hannánoi khitháïŭ; bisurni gezráu găhai' Dal'ugăbáng". Dŭíni modai, Snàpmároi, Bu'rágăkhai", Bírá bífar máni modai danga. Bisurnŭ dáusá * bá fáreo † [A.] árŭ halá ‡ lagainánoi gázi § zang fuzibásŭ, ‖ mànsŭíkhô hambá gárŭ, hannánoi khitháïŭ.

15.—KACHÁRI THEORY OF THUNDER AND LIGHTNING.

Ágláiáu sásè rázá dangman, árŭ bíhá hôásá sásè, hingzháusá sásè, dangman. Hôásáni náu Ráoná, hingzháusáni náu Ráoni dangman. Lásè lásè bísur gădedʹ záabá Ráonáiá gágai binánáukhônŭ hábá khlàmnŭ ¶ nàmainai. Sànsè Ráonáiá rŭnŭïáu ** tháhoinai. Amphárc bíni bifáiá ikhàm zánŭ nàmaibá manákhŭísè, mánathŭ bí rŭnŭïáu thánákhô bifáiá mithiákhaúman ††. Amphá bíni sásè bándiá rŭnŭïáu nunánoi rázáni sĭgángáu khithánaisŭí; abánŭ rázáiá thángnánoi sanghoinaisŭí, balŭi,

---

* "Dáu-sá:" "dáu, fowl; sá" (opposed to "má") diminutive affix [A.—Poáli], a chick, chicken.

Cf. "Dŭí-má," a large river; the Brahmaputra.

"Dŭí-sá," a small river, rivulet, streamlet.

"Mai-má," the {larger } kinds of rice [A.—Bor dhán].

"Mai-sá," ,, {smaller} ,, ,, [A.—Horu dhán].

† "Fáreo" [A.—Pársá], pigeons.

‡ "Halá," oil-lamp (chirágh), used in worship.

§ "Gázi," a mixture of rice (chául) and pulse (máh) steeped in water until it is soft, and then presented in worship to the deities.

‖ "Fuzibá-sŭ" [A.—Pujá kare zadi], if they worship; "sŭ," euphonic.

¶ "Hábá khlàm-nŭ," to marry,—used of the bridegroom (*uxorem ducere*).

** "Rŭ-nŭ," out-house in which rice is pounded with the "dheki;" guest-house.

†† "Mithi-á-khaúman," an unusual form of the negative verb, "mithinŭ," to understand; probably pluperfect;—"had not understood."

"Afá, nangnu ma nanggô? Háthi nánggôbá, háthi hŭgan; gorai nánggôbá, gorai hŭgan; thêobo [A.] nang manáu dukhu dá khàm," hannánoi khithánaisŭí. Abá Ráonáiá hannaisŭí, "Ángnŭ múngbo nángá; nang sŭmai lábásŭ áng khithágan." Amphá bifáiá múngbo uphai [A.] manikhai sŭmai lánánoi khithánaisŭí, "Nangnŭ zikhônŭ nánggô, bíkhônŭ hŭgan." Hanbá Ráonáiá bungnaisŭí, "Ángnŭ Ráonikhô hábá khàmnánoi hŭ; abásŭ áng mikhàm dŭí langgan." Abá bifáiá bibaidi khoráng khnánánoi manáu zábrásin dukhu mannaisŭí. Amphára bifáiá guninánoi sŭmai lánaikhai hábá khlàmnánoi hŭnŭ zathan [A.] khlàmnaisŭí; kintu bê khorángákhô Ráonini sĭgángáu khithánŭ bádá [A.] hŭnai; bínikhai ráubo khithái'-ákhŭí"sè. Amphá Ráoniá mairang sunŭ thángbá dŭígáthánáu* sásè burú'ïá Ráoniniáu sangnaisŭí, balŭí, "Nangsurhá má záadang?" Abá Ráoniá khithánaisŭí, "Zangfrá ádáhá hábá záagan." Árŭ burú'ïá hannaisŭí, "Máunithŭ † hingzháusá zang hábá záanŭ?" Ráoniá bungnaisŭí, "Áng khithánŭ háiá." Abánŭ burú'ïá hannaisŭí, balŭí, "Ai, nang zangsŭ hábá záanŭnŭ." Árŭ Ráoniá hannaisŭí, "Ai, bê khoráng thik ná?" hannanoi sangbá, burú'ïá sŭmai lánaisŭí. Abá Ráoniá akhrangsáu bir'lángnai"sŭí,‡ árŭ Ráunikhô birlángnai nunánoi Ráonáiábo guzarinánoi hasŭ'lángnai"sŭí.‡ Bíkhônŭ mànsŭífrá akhà khrŭm'niákhô"nŭ ‖ "Ráoná guzaridang" hannánoi

---

* "Dŭí-gáthán-áu," Kachári word, "dŭí" (water), compounded with a Hindu word "ghát" (the initial aspirate being dropped in composition) in the locative case. [A.—Pánir ghátat.]

† "Maú-ni-thŭ:" "maŭ" = "maúhá," where? "ni," sign of possessive case; "thŭ," affix expressing astonishment and enquiry; "of what place then? whence?"

‡ "Bir' / "Hasŭ' } láng-nai"-sŭí," { flew away. / ran after, pursued. } Roots compounded with the intensive particle, "láng" (*continued* action).

‖ "Akhá khrŭm'-ni-á-khô"-nŭ," present participle of the verb "akhá khrŭm-nŭ," with noun-ending, "á," attached, used as a noun in objective case; "nŭ," euphonic affix. ("Akhá khrŭm-nŭ," to thunder; "Akhá mablíb-nŭ," to lighten.)

bungŭ; árŭ Ráoni khàṭlángnánoi thàp naifinbá* bíni măkhángá ât baidi nuïŭ, bíkhônŭ akhá mablíbnai hanŭ; Bâṛâfrá eroi bhábiŭ.

16.—MARRIAGE CEREMONIES.

Zaihá fĭsá danga, bíni bimá bifáiá, bí gĭdít záabá, bínŭ hingzháu sangnŭ lági khoráng záaïŭ; árŭ zainiáu hingzháusá nuïŭ, bíkhô nainŭ lági zaú sangŭ. Ampháre zaú záabá hingzháusáni nŭïáu lángŭ. Árŭ zaú langbánŭ boi hingzháusáni bimá bifáiá sangŭ, balŭí, "Nangsur mánŭ zaú lábdang?" Abá hôásáni bimá bifáiá bungŭ, balŭí, "Khoráng̀áu danga, mànsŭíni nŭïáu mànsŭí thángŭ, árŭ masaúni nŭïáu masaú thángŭ; dá nangsurhá· hingzháusá hŭnŭ lagá [A.] dang hannánoi khnádang; nangsur hŭnŭ khusi [A.] dangbá,† hŭnŭ hágaú," erŭí hanŭ. Bínifrá hingzháusáni bimá bifáiá bungŭ, "Zangfarni fĭsáiá nangsurnŭ má máunánoi záhŭgan; ná gudnŭ rangá, ikhàm sangnŭ rangá: áluri hannánoi básiábá nangsurni khusi," erŭí hanbá, hôásáni bimá bifáiá goitháu kháunŭ‡ khànthirá khàmnánoi fáïŭ. Árŭ bínifrai goi fàthoi zŭ khàmnánoi khànthirá khánai dináu goi, fàthoi, ásán árŭ zaú bànnè lánánoi gámini hingzháu, hôá boibo thángŭ; khintu abá baralá árŭ bándi mànsŭí thángnŭ maná; mánathŭ boi sangnai garákhibo baralá bá bándi záanŭ hágaú; bínikhai baralá árŭ bándi hingzháu thángnŭ maná. Bínifrá hingzháusáni nŭïáu

---

* "Nai-fin-bá:" "nainŭ," to look; "fin," affix denoting *repeated* action (*Cf.* "Fá-fin-nŭ," to turn back), "when she keeps looking back repeatedly."

† "Dang-bá," an unusual form of the verb; "bá" (sign of subjunctive mood) being attached to the substantive verb, "dang" (be). "Khusi dang-bá," if it be your pleasure.

‡ "Goitháu kháu-nŭ," to cut open the tamul-nut,—a formal act, indicating the acceptance by the bride's parents of the proposal of marriage made by those of the bridegroom expectant.

manhoibá goi kháunánoi boibo záiŭ; árŭ zaúkhô sítnánoi langŭ. Unáu zaú langkhángbá hôáni fàtsi sásè nísilá árŭ khoráng gărang nainánoi, "Báru"* fàthiŭ [A.]; árŭ hingzháufarni fàtsibo sásè nísilá árŭ khoráng gărang nainánoi, "Báru," fàthiŭ [A.]; árŭ boi bárukhô goi bigur báhŭnánoi masáhŭiŭ;† abá bisurkhô mithihŭiŭ, balŭí, "Bê nŭnè mànsŭíá hingzháu sangnai khoráng nangsur mithi; mobábá gàrzlaibá‡ nangsur hákhi [A.] záanŭ nánggan" hannánoi khitháiŭ. Abánifrai bísur biái biáni‖ samanda [A.] láiŭ. Árŭ basaráu [A.] hôásáni bimá bifáiá háli hágàrbá, mai hákhángbá, árŭ Boiságŭbá,§ bê manthàm thithiáu zaú bànsè bànsè lángnŭ nánggô; lángábá bårå àsár ulthá [A.] záaiŭ. Ampháre basarsè bá basarsè khaisè thánánoi hingzháusáni bifánŭ omá záhŭiŭ; abá boi báru árŭ gámini barai barai mànsŭí gåthå gathai lingnánoi hôásáni nŭáu thángŭ. Bínifrá bísur manhoibánŭ zaú sítnánoi hŭŭí tháiŭ. Unáu omá háthàṭnŭ far [A.] záabá hingzháusáni bifáiá sásè khoráng gărang nainánoi boi báru zang omákhô nainŭ thinŭ. Abá bísur thaiṛŭ thàkháni omábá§ thaibáiáu dànnánoi dinŭ. Bínifrá ikhàm zaú langnánoi akhá naisŭí násŭí¶ faráu bá fungzáni boi ománi findá mannè árŭ zaú bànsè haṛŭ. Amphá bísur boi ománi findákhô gadánánoi khurmáfarnŭ árŭ

---

* "Báru," the official, chosen for the occasion, who acts both as witness and merry-maker during the ceremonies of betrothal.

† "Bá-hŭ-nŭ," to place on the back as a load or burden.
"Masá-hŭï-ŭ" ("masá-nŭ" + "hŭ-nŭ"), to make to dance.

‡ "Gàr-zlai-bá:" "gàr-nŭ," to leave; "zlai," word indicating reciprocal action; "bá," subjunctive mood;—"if they leave each other."

‖ "Biái biá," terms expressing the relationship between the parents of newly betrothed people.

§ "Boiságŭ-bá," "Omá-bá," for "Boiságŭ." "Omá." — + "Záabá;" subj. mood of "záanŭ," to be, become; when *Boisákh* has come; "when it is a pig (of the value of six rupees.")

¶ "Akhá naisŭí násŭí," in the early morning. [A.—Rátipuái.]

gamini mansúnü bángai bangai hüiü. Árü bínifrá basarsèsü thánánoi bimánü omá záhüiü; abábo omá findá árü zaú bànsè láboïü. Unáu bor bhárni omá záhüiü, abá nünènibo khurmá gâthâ gathai zü záanü nánggô, árü zai sangdang, boi gâthâiábo thángnü nánggô; bí thángábá omá záhünü háiá; áglá omá záhünaiáu bí thángnü nángá; khintu bor bhárni omá záhübá thángábá záiá.

Amphá bor bhárni omá záhükhángbá,* hábá khàmnü zathan [A.] khàmü, árü goi, fàthoi, omá, mairang, sangkhrè árü zaú bífar màni, hábáiáu zi zi nánggô, boikhôbo zü khàmü. Unáu bêfar zü záabá hingzháusáni bimá bifánü báthrá [A.] hüṛü. Arü khoiná [A.] lainü lági bårå, arthát [A.] hôásáfrá sikhlá árü burúï hingzháu thángü. Árü hingzháusáni bimá bifáiábo gámini hingzháu lingnánoi fïsázü zang hüṛü: abá hingzháusáiá gànüí † zumüí † ankhàrnánoi bimá, bifá, bimáiang,‡ árü bimádoifarkhô ‡ khulúmü. Amphá hingzháufrá boi hingzháusákhô gezêr′ khàmnánoi láboïü; árü bí gábbá bísur buzáïü [A.] balüí, "Ai, dá gáb; mánü gábdang? mábá nang balü málaini nüïáu thángnü gnáng záadang ná? hingzháu zanam [A.] lábá boibo málaini nüáu thángnü nánggô. Dá nang dá gáb; mábrüíhai gàhámüí nü záagan, bíkhôsü sinthi [A.] Árü nangni hôáiá hábá máunánoi dukhunifrá ikhàm ukhúïnánoi faibá, árü düí gángnánoi faibá, nang ikhàm düí hünü lági gamfàthinánoi dá thá," erüí hannánoi buzáïü [A.] Amphá daráni nü manhoibá, daráni fàtsi thánai

* "Zá-hü-kháng-bá:" "zá-nü," to eat; "hü-nü," to give; "kháng," word indicating completeness; "bá," subjunctive affix;—having finished feasting (on the pig.)

† "Gàn-üí," "Zum-üí," } to put on the { "dhuti" (loin-cloth.) "bor kápar" (upper garment); to clothe completely. (Participial adverbs from "gàn-nü," "zum-nü.")

‡ "Bimáiang" [A.—Zethá] "Bimádoi" [A.—Dodai] } father's { elder younger } brother.

hingzháufrá lámá nánglúiáu khoináni [A.] árŭ bíni lagŭni hingzháufarni átheng sunŭ nánggô; unáu átheng sukhángbá, khoinákhô árŭ bíni lagŭni hingzháufarkhô gubun nŭiáu dinhŭiŭ.* Ampháre boibo ikhàm zánánoi árŭ zaú langnánoi fungzáni thángŭ. Bínifrá fainai manáiáu áru gámini mànsŭí lingnánoi ikhàm zaú langhŭiŭ;* bíkhônŭ "háthá suni" hŭnai hanŭ; abánifrá boi gåthåsá árŭ hingzháusá sánèbo lagŭsŭ tháiŭ. Bí horsè thánánoi fungáu daráni bimá bifáiá khoináni nŭiáu zaú lánánoi thángŭ; abá hingzháusánŭ khurmáfrá zi zi hŭiŭ, bíkhô láboiŭ. Árŭ bísur hôá hingzháu sánèbo Boiságbá † Boiságbá † zaú lángnŭ nánggô; abá bimá annánoi khurúi bá thorsi bá omá bá dáu harŭ.

17.—FUNERAL RITES.

Bårâfrá mànsŭí thoibá nŭni mànsŭífur dikhàr khàmnánoi gábŭ, árŭ khaisè mànsŭiá ban dànhŭiŭ; unáu bankhô rŭgánánoi ‡ dŭísá zingáu lángŭ. Ampháre ban rŭgákhángbá gŭthoikhô lángnŭ zathan [A.] khàmŭ. Árŭ gŭthoikhô sethеláu dihannánoi thukhúiŭ.‖ Árŭ khåråáu mådamáubo tháu hŭiŭ; árŭ hí gadàn gànhŭiŭ. Bínifrá nŭni mànsŭífrá árŭ gámini mànsŭífrábo zaihá zaihá khusi [A.] záaiŭ, bísur ikhàm bángai, zaú bángai, árŭ dŭí bángai daúöŭ.§ Unáu gŭthoikhô bànnánoi dŭísá zingáu lángŭ. Ampháre banfarkhô zábnánoi bíni sáu gŭthoikhô dinŭ, árŭ gŭthoini sáubo ban bángai zábŭ. Nŭni mànsŭiá hakti [A.] thábá darbi bángai

---

* "Din / "Lang { hŭiŭ } din-nŭ," / lang-nŭ," { + "hŭ-nŭ," to give, } causative forms of the respective simple verbs.

† "Boiság-bá," "Boiság" + "záabá;" (subj. mood of "záa-nŭ," to be, become); "when *Boiság* has come," *i.e.*, in the month of *Boisákh*, year by year.

‡ "Rŭ-gá-nŭ," to lift and carry loads (of firewood, &c.)

‖ "Thukhúï-nŭ," / "Dugúï-nŭ," } to bathe { another. / one's self.

§ "Daú-nŭ," to feed others with one's own hand; "Zá-hŭ-nŭ," give others food in a general sense.

hŭiŭ, darbi hŭnŭ háiábá foisá [A.] gadbrŭí hŭiŭ. Bínifrá hôábá khanbá, hingzháubá khansní gidingnánoi ád lagáiŭ. Unáu găthoikhô sáukhángbá, sáunai tháuniáu besar fŭnánoi mànsŭífrá dugúinánoi fáiŭ. Nŭiáu safaibá gâthâ gathai boibo nárzè găkhá ná fisá zang bángai bángai záiŭ. Árŭ dáu másè buthátnánoi sangzáiŭ; bíkhô "báli gătháng* hŭnai" hanŭ. Abá bíkhô zánánoi zaúfar langnánoi gámini mànsŭífrá nŭiáu thángsŭí. Bínifrá hôábá sànbá, hingzháusábá sànsní thánánoi suá [A.] gàrnŭ zathan khàmŭ; árŭ goi, fathoi, zaú árŭ omá zi zi nánggô màni futhumnánoi, khurmá árŭ gámini mànsŭífrá faibá, manáiáu găthoini làgi fithá [A.] khàmnánoi boi horsè màni udúá lábá zaú langnánoi, găthoinŭ, hôábá thaibà, hingzháusábá thaisní, fithá khàmŭ. Unáu akhánaibá, boi fithá árŭ thorsi gángsè, khurúi thaisè, dábar gángsè, árŭ foisá befarkhô lángnánoi dŭísá zingáu abuthá [A.] ôá hásung zang báöŭ.† Bínifrá nŭíáu fainánoi omá háthàrŭ, abá suá thángsŭí. Amphá, boi omákhô măzángŭí sáunánoi bí ománi khámihárákhô [A.] bigúr, mâdam, begeng zang biseng‡ háiŭ, bíkhônŭ omá biseng‖ hanŭ. Bí bisengkhô hôábá sengbá khàmŭ, hingzháusábá sengsní khàmŭ. Bíni unáu tháu zang sèrŭ.§ Amphá bêlá láhaibá¶ tháuni lítnánoi átheng gnáng khàmflaiákhô măzángŭí sunánoi bŭnánoi** laizaú gángsè bíni sáunŭ bŭiŭ. Bihánŭ

* "Báli găthàng;" a technical expression, indicating that the guests and other attendants at a funeral (cremation) are freed from ceremonial impurity, though the family of the deceased are *not* so.

† "Bá-nŭ" [A.—Ág bárhôá], to lay down (present) formally gifts as offerings at worship, funerals, &c.

‡ "Biseng" ("seng"), strips—not wholly dissevered—into which the sides of a pig are cut, to be presented as offerings.

‖ "Omá biseng" for "ománi biseng;" sign of possessive case ("ni") often omitted in composition.

§ "Sèr-nŭ," to cook in oil [A.—Bházibo].

¶ "Bêlá láhaibá" [A.—Gadhuli], the latter part of the day—just before sunset.

** "Bŭ-nŭ," to place, spread out (leaves, &c.) at meals, worship, &c.

hí gadan, thàkha, khuroi, thorsi, oma biseng,* zaú befarkhô thulusini dŭí lánánoi sàtnánoi † báöŭ. Bínifrá báukhángbá omá bisengkhô, aru zaúkhô gárŭ. Amphá hí, thàkhá, khuroi, thorsi befarkhô, thulisini dŭí zang sàtnánoi láfá'finŭ. Ampháre sethlá [A.] sípnánoi ‡ ikhàm khutnŭ ‖ lai bŭnŭ thanŭ. Amphá lai bŭbá sethlá gezráunu zau zorásè, amphá ikhàm háthánè, mêgang háthánè, amphá mairang donsè, árŭ bíohánŭ ádlisènibo hiki gatthàmni foisá dinnanoi ág'barai"nánoi [A.] bor bíŭ. Ampháre boibo bor husuí. Abániá bor hŭblá nŭni hôá sásè sáne mansuua anthu [A.] khárinánoi [A.] khulúmŭ; khu'lúmnai"nifra uthinanoi donkhô ákhauau lánánoi nŭfàtsi makháng khàmnánoi bí donni mairang zang foisá zang muthá márinánoi lasuí lasuı unfàtsi sat-haṛŭ; amphá nŭiáu dinhoisuí, amphá mànsuufrá ikhàm zasuı. Amphá ikhàm zákháng langkhangnánoi boi zaú zorasèkhô langnanoi boi foisákhô nŭni mànsŭínŭ hŭfáfinŭ; bêohánŭ nŭni mànsŭíá boi foisákhô khaifáhá láiŭ, khaifáhá laıa; laıaba gamini mànsŭífránŭ ràinnánoi láiŭ; amphá nŭ gai gai thángsŭí.

---

* "Omá biseng" for "ománi biseng;" sign of possessive case ("ni") often omitted in composition.

† "Sàt-nŭ," to sprinkle.

‡ "Síp-nŭ," to sweep.

‖ "Khut-nŭ," to divide.

VOCABULARY.

THIS vocabulary will, it is believed, be found to contain m of the words used in the foregoing reading lessons, with two exc tions, *viz.*, (1), words obviously adopted from the Assame Hindustáni, &c., which the student will at once recognize ; a (2), words in everyday use—*e.g.*, personal pronouns, numera &c., with which the learner's study of the Grammar will alrea have made him familiar.

The *order* followed is (1), that of the vowels as given in m English Grammars, *i.e.*, a, (á), e, i, o, u ; and (2), that of the co sonants as arranged in the English alphabet, certain unnecesse letters (c, j, &c.,) being omitted.

The words are for the most part given in their simplest a shortest form, with the exception of the verb, which invarial appears in the Infinitive mood, the characteristic "sign" "n (="to") of that mood being separated from the root by a hyph

In order to assist the learner, the meaning of the Kach words is given both in Assamese and in English—the Assamese, well as the Kachári, words being spelt *phonetically*, without ref ence to Etymology.

Kachári.	*Assamese.*	*English.*
Abá Abánŭ	... Têtiá, tente	... Then.
Akhá (nakhá*)	... Barakhún	... Rain.
Akhrangsá	... Ákáh	... Sky, firmament.
Amphá Ampháre	... Pásê, písat	... Then, afterwards.
An-nŭ	... Prem kará	... To love.
Anthai Anthaiblá	... Bá, náïbá	... Either, or.
Azainŭ	... Hadai, horbadai ...	Always, ever.
Ádàr	... Áhár, khôá bastu ..	Food, bread.

Kachári.	*Assamese.*	*English.*
Agar-nŭ (Hágàr-nŭ)	... Êrá	... Leave off, desist; forgive.
Ágdá	... Hôn	... Right (hand).
Áglaiá	... Ágê	... Before.
Ásán	... Kháru	... Bangle; ornament worn on wrist by women.
Ásu	... Nakh	... Claw, nail.
Átheng	... Bhori	... Foot.
Ekrab	... Khahatá	... Wrinkled.
Em	... Dhári	... Matting, bed.
Émáu	... Darab	... Yeast, condiment used in preparing *mådh*.
Erŭíhai	... Ene	... So, thus.
Ikhàm (mikhàm*)	Bhát	... Rice (cooked).
Inzat	... Nigoni	... Mouse.
Inzat bonggá	... Endur	... Rat.
Oma	... Gáhuri	... Pig, hog.
Ôá	... Bánh	... Bamboo.
Udoi	... Pêt	... Abdomen.
Udú-nŭ	... Húá	... To sleep.
Ukhúī-nŭ	... Bhôk lagá	... To be hungry.
Ukhunduí	... Dhûá	... Smoke.
Unáu	... Písê	... After, afterwards.
Bá'behá	... Kôt	... Where ?
Baidi	... Ene	... Thus, so.
Balŭ	... Kêwal, màthon	... Only.
Ban	... Khori	... Firewood.
Bangfang	... Gás (gách)	... Tree.
Baralá (dunggúá)..	Baralá	... Widower.
Báhŭnŭ	... Bôká lôá (?)	... To carry on the back(?)

* The semi-vowels "m" and "n" are sometimes omitted, sometimes inserted, when used as initials, without any obvious difference of meaning.

Kachári.	*Assamese.*	*English.*
Bándi	Bêti	Maidservant; widow.
Bási-nŭ	Máná	Regard, consider.
Báugàr-nŭ	Páhará	Forget.
Bàn	Bhár	Load.
Bàn-nŭ	Dángá	To lift (as a load.)
Bángai	Alapmán	A little.
Bêgeng	Hár	Bone.
Besar	Horiȧh	Mustard-seed.
Bèsè	Kêītá	How many?
Bèsèbáng	Kimán	How much?
Biáunŭ	Têtiá	Then, there (*lit.*, in that)
Bidaṭ	Mangah, mángsa	Flesh.
Bigúṛ	Sál	Skin, hide.
Bilai	Pát	Leaf (of trees, &c.)
Bímá	Maiki	Female (of animals).
Bizuá	Anta, heh	End, extremity.
Boi Boibo	Átai, hokolô	All.
Buá	Kêwal, màthon	Only.
Bundŭí	Gákhír	Milk.
Bung-nŭ	Bulá	To say, speak.
Bu-thàṭ-nŭ	Márá (prán márá).	To kill (by beating).
Bhár (A.)	Bhár	Burden, load.
Bràp-nŭ	Khang kará	To be angry.
Dŭí	Zal, páni	Water.
Dŭí-má	Nadi	River (large).
Dŭí-sá	Nadi, noi	River (small), rivulet.
Darbi	Sôn (hôn)	Gold.
Dábar	Soriá	Water-vessel (wooden).
Dá Dánŭ	Êtiá	Now.
Dáng-nŭ	Sôá	To touch.
Dàlai	Tháni, dál	Branch, bough (of trees).

Kachári.	*Assamese.*	*English.*
Dàn̊-nŭ	... Kátá	... To cut.
Dihañ-nŭ	... Uliôá	... To bring out.
Dikháng-nŭ	... Tulá	... To lift up.
Dikhàr	... Dukh	... Grief, sorrow.
Din-hŭnŭ	... Thôá, thoi díá	... To place, lay out, set out in order (causative).
Din-nŭ	... Thôá	... To place.
Dor	... Duár′	... Door, gate.
Fakhrá sikhrá	... Dhekiá patiá	... Striped (of tigers, &c.)
Farang̊-nŭ	... Hikhôá	... To teach.
Fàn-nŭ	... Besá	... To sell.
Fàt (fàtsi)	... Phál, pôn	... Side, direction.
Fŭ-nŭ	... Hisá (?)	... To sow rice, vegetables, &c.
Findá	... Phêrá	... Thigh.
Fĭsí-nŭ	... Bhízôá	... To steep.
Fĭsá (fsá)	... Lorá, sôáli	... Child, offspring, descendants.
Fithikhá	... Photiká	... Spirit distilled from *mådh*.
Fudúng-nŭ	... Phutôá, garm kará	To boil, cause to boil.
Fungzáni	... Rátipuá	... In the morning, early.
Futhúm̊-nŭ	... Gotôá; zama kará	To gather, collect.
Găbáng	... Harah, anek	... Much, many.
Gad (gat)	... ...	... (Classifying numeral prefix).
Gada	... Dingi	... Neck.
Gădat (gădít, gădet, &c.)	Bor, dángar	... Great, large.
Gădá-nŭ	... Dukhor dukhore kátá.	To cut up (flesh, &c.,) into pieces.
Găfát	... Zúngá	... Sharp-pointed, acute.

Kachári.	*Assamese.*	*English.*
Găfút°	... Bôgá	... White.
Găhai	... Sápor, horu	... Short (of height), small.
Găhàm	... Bhál	... Good.
Găkhá	... Títá	... Bitter.
Gălau	... Dighal	... Long.
Gamfàthi-nŭ	... Gaf kará	... To be proud.
Ganthang	... Nák	... Nose.
Gasam̒	... Kala	... Black.
Găsang-nŭ	... Thíá hoi thaká	... To stand upright.
Găthai	... Eke báre, humoli...	At once; altogether.
Gătháu	... Húád, mithai	... Sweet
Găthaú	... Dâ	... Deep.
Găthár	... Husi (suchi)	... Pure (in Hindu ceremonial sense).
Găzaú°	... Dighal, sarah	... Tall.
Găzá	... Rangá, lál	... Red.
Găzáng	... Zár lagá	... Cold.
Gá-nŭ	... Gosakôá	... To tread upon.
Gáuthàṛ-nŭ	... Guliôá	... To shoot to death.
Gáb-nŭ	... Kándá, krandan kará.	To weep, cry.
Gádoi la-nu	... Lêti lôá	... To wallow (of hogs, &c.)
Gámi	... Gáon̲ (grám)	... Village.
Gáng-nŭ	... Piá lagá	... To be thirsty.
Gángsŭ	... Gan̲h	... Grass.
Gár-nŭ	... Erá	... To leave, quit, give up.
Gázri	... Moilá, kurup	... Dirty, ugly.
Gàgai	... Ápôn, etá etákoi...	Each, every (distributive), own.
Ganda	... Gâr	... Rhinoceros.
Gàn-nŭ	... Pindhá	... To put on clothing (*dhuti*).
Gelê-nu	... Dhemáli kará	... To play.
Gezráu	... Mazat	... In the midst.

Kachári.		*Assamese.*		*English.*
Giding-nŭ	...	Ghuri ghuri zôá	...	To go round.
Gí-nŭ	...	Bhoi kará	...	To fear, be afraid.
Gaglai-nŭ	...	Pará	...	To fall down.
Goi fàthoi	...	Tàmal pán	...	Betel-nut and *pán*.
Gú-ár	...	Bahal'	...	Broad.
Gúbún	...	Anya, án	...	Other.
Guḍ-nŭ	...	Ásorá	...	To scratch, tear, claw.
Gudúng	...	Garm	...	Warm, hot.
Guni-nŭ [A.]	..	Ganan kará	...	To count, reckon.
Gundúï	...	Pithágauri	...	Pounded rice-flour.
Gunthútri	...	Dhuthuri	...	Jaw, lips (of animals).
Gurúï	...	Naram ; dhílá	...	Soft.
Gusúng	...	Suti, horu	...	Short, &c. (of stature).
Gushthoi	...	Ôth	...	Lips (of men).
Guzúri-nŭ	...	Siôrá, ringiôá	...	To roar, bellow.
Ham-nŭ	...	Dhará	...	To catch, seize, hold.
Haṅ-nŭ	...	Bulá	...	To say, call, speak.
Hasŭ-nŭ	...	Khedá	...	To chase, pursue.
Hatbai	...	Dêo di	...	Jump, frisk (of lambs).
Haṭ-nŭ	...	Pathïô'á	...	To send.
Hábá máu-nŭ	...	Kám kará	...	To work.
Hábá khàm-nŭ	...	Biá kará	...	To marry.
Hágrá	...	Hábi, jangal	...	Jungle, waste land.
Háli oi-nŭ	...	Hál bôá	...	To plough.
Hásung	...	Sungá	...	Bamboo tube (*sungá*).
Háthá	...	Biá kará bhôz	...	Feast given at betrothals, &c.
Háthai	...	Dánt	...	Tooth.
Háthàṭ-nŭ	...	Káti márá	...	To kill (by cutting).
Hŭ-nŭ	...	Díá	...	To give.
Heloi!	...	Herá!	...	Oh! ho there! (voc. case.)
Hingzháusá	...	Tíri, tír'otá	...	Woman.

Kachári.		*Assamese.*		*English.*
Hí'	...	Kápâr	...	Cloth, clothing.
Hor	...	Ráti	...	Night.
Hung-grí-nŭ	...	Hu'orá	...	To bear in mind, remember.
Khaise	...	Kônô kônô	...	Some.
Khâifaihá	...	Kônô kônôr	...	Of some (possessive case of above).
Khaman	...	Núm, lúm	...	Wool, hair (of animals).
Khamsi	...	Endhár	...	Darkness.
Khan	...	Bêli, bár, hamoi	...	Occasion, time.
Khàthi	...	Ôsar	...	Near.
Khàmflai	...	Pírá	...	Bench, seat, stool.
Khànthirá	...	Níam	...	Agreement, covenant.
Khàṭ-nŭ	...	Lor márá	...	To run.
Khàṭ-láng-nŭ	...	Lor mári zôá	...	To run away.
Khåmá	...	Kán	...	Ear.
Khårå	...	Múr	...	Head.
Khithá-nŭ	...	Kôá	...	To speak, say.
Khoráng	...	Kathá, bíbaran	...	Word, speech, proverb.
Khorblá khorblá	...	Dobalá dobal	...	Pitted, indented.
Khurúi	...	Báti	...	Brass drinking vessel.
Khurmá	...	Mittra, sináki	...	Friend, acquaintance.
Khulúm-nŭ	...	Hêwá (pujá) kará.		To worship, do reverence.
Khúgá	...	Mukh	...	Mouth.
Khlàm-nŭ	...	Kará	...	To do, to work, carry out.
Khná-nŭ	...	Huná	...	To hear.
Laizaú	...	Pát bisêsh	...	The leaf of a certain shrub.
Lai ba-nŭ	...	Pát pårá	...	To lay out leaves in order (for a feast, &c.)

Kachári.	*Assamese.*	*English.*
Ladá-nŭ	... Gotôá	... To collect, gather.
Làmá	... Bát, áli	... Road, path, highway.
Làmá nanglá	... Bát ghar	.... Porch ; vestibule.
Lá-nŭ	... Áná	... To bring.
Láng-nŭ	... Níá ; loi-zôá	... To take away.
Lànzaí	... Nigúr (nêgúr)	... Tail.
Ling-nŭ	... Mátá	... To call.
Lít-nŭ (líd-nŭ)	... Lekhá ; lípá	... To write, plaster, paint.
Lubúī-nŭ	... Lôbh kará	... To covet, desire.
Mai	... Dhán	... Rice, paddy.
Mairang	... Sáúl	... Rice (husked).
Mablíp-nŭ	... Bizuli díá	... To lighten (lightning).
Makháng	... Mukh	... Face, expression.
Makhná	... Bhêtê	... A plant the leaves of which are used in preparing *mådh.*
Manàm-nŭ	... Gandhá	... To smell.
Man-nŭ	... Pôá	... To find, experience.
Má ?	... Kí ?	... What ?
Mábá	... Kíbá	... Something.
Máu-nŭ	... Kám kará	... To work.
Málai	... Anya	... Other.
Mámàr	... Begai	... Quickly.
Mángkhor	... Kabar, moidám	... Grave, tomb.
Mánathŭ	... Tátê, káran	... Wherefore, therefore.
Máthili	... Tekeli.	... Round, shallow earthen ware vessel, used in preparing *mådh.*
Mådam	... Gá, horil	... Body.
Mêgan̈	... Sôku	... Eye.
Mendá	... Mêrság	... Sheep.
Mikhàm (ikhàm)	.. Bhát	... Rice (cooked).
Mithi-nŭ	... Buzá	... To understand.

Kachári.		*Assamese.*		*English.*
Mobábá	...	Kêtiábá	...	Sometimes.
Mobábrŭíbá	...	Kônobá môtê	...	In some way or other, somehow.
Mosá	...	Bágh	...	Tiger.
Mosaú'°	...	Gôru	...	Cow.
Mozáng'	...	Hundor, sáfá	...	Beautiful, clean.
Mu	...	Dêrh hát	...	An arm-length (used in measurement).
Mudoi (udoi)	...	Horu, sôtá	...	Small, little.
Múdú-nŭ (udú-nŭ)		Húá	...	To sleep.
Mugúī-nŭ	...	Ghin kará	...	To hate.
Múli	...	Darab, dáwai	...	Medicine.
Múngbo	...	Kíbá	...	Something, anything.
Muthá	...	Muthi	...	A handful of *dhán* with *straw* attached.
Nai-nŭ	...	Sôá, dekhá	...	To look, see.
Nai hat!	...	Soásôn!	...	Look! look!
Namai-nŭ	...	Khuzá	....	To wish, desire.
Ná	...	Más (mách)	...	Fish.
Náu	...	Nám	....	Name.
Nâng-gô	...	Láge, proiozan	....	It is necessary, must.
Nâng-á	...	Ná láge	....	Must not, needless.
Nàrzè	...	Mará pát	....	Hemp.
Nŭ	...	Ghor	....	House.
Nisilá	...	Niláz	...	Shameless, bold.
Nu-nŭ	...	Dekhá	...	To see.
Rai-nŭ	...	Kôá	...	To speak, say.
Rang-nŭ	...	Záná	...	To know, perceive.
Razá	...	Dáth	...	Thick, dense.
Ráubo	...	Kônô	...	Anyone.
Ràn-nŭ	...	Hukhá	...	To dry up (neuter).

Kachári.	*Assamese.*	*English.*
Sau-nu	... (1) Dhán khunda, (2) kilôá.	To (1) husk rice, (2) pound, bruise (with the hand).
Sabai	... Máh, mátikalai ...	Pulse, grain.
Sab-nŭ	... Sákí sôà ...	Taste by sucking.
Safai-nŭ	... Bhángá ...	To break.
Sangkhrŭí	... Lún, nimak ...	Salt.
Sang-nŭ (1)	... Hizôá ...	To cook.
——— (2)	... Bhuká ...	— bark (of dogs, &c.)
——— (3)	... Hudhá ...	— ask, question.
Sáu-nŭ	... Purá, zúï lagôá ...	To set on fire, kindle.
Sár	... Bolawanta, sôká ...	Strong, keen.
Sát-hŭ-nŭ	... Hisôá ...	To cause to pour out (water, &c.)
Sàgremá	... Bázi ...	Barren (of animals).
Sán	... Bêli, hurjya, dín ...	The sun, day.
Sŭímá	... Kukur ...	Dog.
Sŭmai	... Hopot ...	Oath.
Sŭm-nŭ	... Bhizoa ...	To soak, steep one's self
Sŭ-nŭ	... Homôá ...	To fill vessels (*kalsi*, *sungá*, &c.) with water.
Sesá	... Hohá pohú ...	Hare.
Sikháu	... Sôr ...	Thief, robber.
Singáu	... Tolot ...	Under.
Sigángáu	... Ágê ...	Before, in front,
Sít-nŭ	... Dhálá ...	To pour water, &c., from a *kalsi*, &c.
Suthàr-nŭ	... Bindhai prán márá	To kill by stabbing.
Sri sri!	... Mone mone thá! ...	Hush ! silence !
Thafá	... Zák, mêr	Flock, herd.
Thañ-nŭ	... Merôá ...	To roll up and enclose anything in cloth, &c.

Kachári.	*Assamese.*	*English.*
Tháu*	... Têl	... Oil (vegetable)
Tháuni	... Thai	... Place, site.
Thá-nŭ	... Tháká	... To stay, remain.
Tháng-nŭ	... Zôá	... To go.
Thángnai	... Ziá	... Living (adj.)
Tháp	... Begai, ghane ghane	Quickly, repeatedly.
Thàbai-nŭ	... Phurá	... To walk, go forward.
Thŭ-nŭ	... Átá, zúrá	... To suffice, be sufficient.
Thin-nŭ	... Usatôá, salôá	... To urge on, incite.
Thing	... Phàl, pôn	... Side, direction.
Thingkhili	... Tekeli	... Small earthenware vessel for holding *gúr*, &c.
Thíthibai-nŭ	... Dekhúá	... To point out, direct.
Thoi	... Tez	... Blood.
Thorsi	... Káhi	.... Brass plate from which rice is eaten at meals.
Zaú	... Mâdh	... *Mâdh*, rice-beer.
Zaúdá	... Kalsi	.... Earthen water-vessel.
Zabam	... Kopál	... Forehead.
Zági-nŭ (A.)	... Zanam pôá	... To be born.
Zŭp-nŭ (zŭb-nŭ)...	Heh pôá, dhukôá..	To cease, end.
Zá-nŭ	... Khôá	... To eat.
Zá hŭ-nŭ	... Khuôá	... To cause to eat, feed.
Zaa-nŭ	... Hôá	.... To be, become.
Záa-hŭ-nŭ	... Hobo díá	.... To cause to be, create.
Záb-nŭ (záp-nŭ)...	Zápi thôá	... To place (books, &c.) in order, one on the other.
Zábrá	... Horoh, anek	... Much, many.
Zŭ { khàm-nŭ	... Gotôá	... To gather, collect.
Zŭ { záa-nŭ	... Gôt hôá	... To be gathered, collected.

* Mezem ... Têl ... Oil (animal).

Kachári.	*Assamese.*	*English.*
Zê ...	Zál ...	Net.
Zeblá ...	Zêtiá ...	When.
Zeblábá ...	Hodai ...	Whenever, always.
Zeraú ...	Zôt, zôte	Where.
Zerehai ...	Zene	As (relative).
Zingáu ...	Kôkhe, kôkhorot....	By the side of, alongside.
Zôbrá ...	Rúgiá, bimár	Sick, invalided.
Zôrá (A.), banzàr	Zor	Torch.
Zum-nŭ* ...	Urá	To put on clothing (*bor kápar*).
Zlá (zălá) ...	Môtá	Male (of birds, &c.)

* Gàn-nŭ ... Pindhá ... To put on the loin-cloth (*dhuti*).